T5-DII-587

THE EVALUATION OF TRAINING IN MENTAL HEALTH

THE EVALUATION OF TRAINING IN MENTAL HEALTH

by

Marcia Guttentag
Harvard University

and

Thomas Kiresuk
Hennepin County Mental Health Service

Madelynn Oglesby
University of Delaware

Jerry Cahn
Graduate School—City University of New York

Behavioral Publications, Inc.
New York

WILLIAM MADISON RANDALL LIBRARY UNC AT WILMINGTON

Library of Congress Catalog Number 74-8506
ISBN: 0-87705-161-5
Copyright © 1975 by Behavioral Publications, Inc.

All rights reserved. No part of this work may be reproduced
or utilized in any form or by any means, electronic or
mechanical, including photocopying, microfilm and recording,
or by any information storage and retrieval system without
permission in writing from the publisher.

BEHAVIORAL PUBLICATIONS, INC.
72 Fifth Avenue
New York, New York 10011

Printed in the United States of America
56789   987654321

Library of Congress Cataloging in Publication Data

Guttentag, Marcia.
    The evaluation of training in mental health.

    Bibliography: p.
    1. Mental hygiene—Study and teaching—Evaluation.
I. Title. [DNLM: 1. Community mental health services
—United States. 2. Evaluation studies. WM18 E92]
RA790.8.G87   362.2'2'07   74-8506

R A 790
. 8
. G 8 7

Contents

135791

Foreword

This book had its origin in the work of the Steering Committee on Training in Community Mental Health. One of the task forces set up by this group dealt with the evaluation of training in community mental health. Among its members were the authors, Guttentag, Kiresuk, Oglesby and Cahn. This book grew out of their report on the evaluation of training in community mental health.

The authors wish to thank their colleagues on the Steering Committee for having given the impetus for their consideration of this topic, and for having enabled them to meet regularly. Most importantly, we thank them for their intellectual input and for their continued emphasis on social, moral and ethical issues in evaluation, emphases which we hope they will find reflected throughout this book.

Part I

APPROACHING THE EVALUATION OF TRAINING

This section presents a method of organizing and conceptualizing the evaluation research task. It can be viewed as a guide to thinking about the various dimensions that must be considered in the evaluation of training. It also offers a tabular presentation of the overall structure, so that it is possible to see how each of the investigated dimensions relates to the others.

1

Conceptualization of the Evaluation Problem

MARCIA GUTTENTAG

Certain basic principles of evaluation have guided the presentation that follows. They underlie the practical methods for evaluation of training which are suggested. These principles can be summarized as follows:

Values: The value positions of this task force include a predisposition to multisystem approaches to evaluation. Methods for the evaluation of training are needed which can guide in the determination of what one asks, whom one asks, how one asks and how one deals with the answers. Evaluation should measure the impact of feedback on the program.

There are other important issues. Evaluation

should be of both process and outcome: e.g., how does the program affect the later behavior of students, of patients and of the community? The design of the evaluation should be related to the goals of the organization. The consequences of both formative and summative feedback and evaluation must be considered. Further, there is a need for feedback to ensure changes in the ongoing program. Most important, the values involved in the training program must be specified and quantified: e.g., to legislators, consumers or trainees.

The most critical general principle of evaluation is that it must be relevant to the consumer and to the decisionmakers of the program. The values of the decisionmakers must be described and quantified. Further, the relationship between evaluation (and evaluation research) and planning, power and decisionmaking in the organization must be specified: e.g., should the evaluator be separate from, or a part of, the organization?

Whenever possible, a micro- to macrosystems approach should be used. Evaluation should begin at the clinical (one-to-one) level and move up to higher social-system levels. At the same time, feedback must be provided from one level to the next.

Managerial systems should be studied as part of the evaluation. Managerial systems can be treated as microsystems, and can be considered from the cost/effectiveness viewpoint. Managerial systems should also be studied for their degree of responsiveness to community needs. Ecological as well as etiological needs should be studied.

The scope of evaluation should be as wide as possible. Therefore, evaluation should begin before the program starts. Evaluation researchers should be involved in the selection of populations, etc. Resource allocation and costs of the program should be a part of the evaluation.

Methods of data collection must be carefully chosen. Obtrusive, and/or unobtrusive and/or archival data can be used in combination or alone. The importance of naturalistic observations should be recognized. Paper and pencil questionnaires and demographic data should not be the sole sources of information utilized.

The discussion of the problem of the evaluation of training which follows is informed by the above principles.

2

The Organization of the Evaluation Research

A general strategy for an evaluation system should accommodate just about any form of educational program, since there are many community mental health philosophies and programs, and this multiplicity should be fostered. Although the problem presents no conceptual difficulty and the solution is straightforward, it is hard to do.

The criticism, "This is to be only more of the same," is one frequently delivered with regard to many evaluation systems that purport to assess new methods. The evaluation may only serve to strengthen the old method. Basic philosophies of those in power determine the objectives and the extent to which they will be carried out. Using base-rate expectations in lieu of formal, explicit declarations of values, one can expect that if white doctors and administrators direct the program and its evaluation, whites will dominate the power structure, traditional sources of income and status will be protected, humanitarian and liberal features will be conspicuous but functionally impotent, males and the existing professions will emerge in control.

The results-oriented evaluator can easily fit into such a design. By focusing attention at the bottom of the administrative system, the top administration avoids evaluation on itself. It is easier to elicit goals and objectives and to devise measures to gauge progress on lower levels of administration. In addition, it is easier to set up ongoing monitoring systems on these lower levels. This serves to lock in the system early, prevent change and ensure control and accountability that is directed from the top downward. In brief, the scope of the evaluation system can be too small.

Therefore, the development of a system that would begin with or at least include a definition and study of the philosophies and constraints imposed by the current power structure, the largest elements of influence operating in the area of training for community mental health, is needed. Without this analysis we are likely to end up with such measures as student satisfaction or course-content analysis unrelated to the larger, real directives of the program. An analogy would be the work done by evaluators of mental retardation services. Very careful studies of relative success rates for different treatments measured in terms of return to the community miss the point that the institution is to keep these people out of the community, out of their homes, maintained at minimal public cost and treated with sufficient humanity to satisfy public conscience.

First, one should define the purpose of the evaluation. Only one possible interpretation of this enterprise has been taken and the outline developed accordingly. Then follows a description of the structure and dynamics of community mental health training. The structural description proceeds from the largest to the smallest units and defines some of the essential components of the system. Dynamics of the system would describe interrelationships among these components. A resource analysis should follow, indicating first, the nature and degree of resources available to the total system; next, the information system, how it relates to the structure and dynamics of the system; then the information system itself, some examples of management information, outcome measurement and reporting systems. An overall summary diagram of this outline is shown in Table 2.1. (See next page.)

I. General Purpose of the Evaluation: A Sample of General Purposes, Goals and Objectives of Various Levels of Abstraction
—To devise an evaluation system which is responsive to organizational and philosophical change—change resulting from within the system findings and rededication resulting from cultural, economic administrative and scientific evaluation outside the system.
—To define the components of operation and

Table 2.1

RELATIONSHIP OF EVALUATION SYSTEM TO
STRUCTURAL ELEMENTS OF MENTAL HEALTH EDUCATION

Evaluation-System Components	Levels of Structure		
	Level I General Public Federal Legislative Federal Executive	Level II Government Administration Academic Administration	Level III Training Centers Service Centers
I. General Purpose of the Evaluation			
II. Structural Definition and Intent of Structure Elements			
III. Dynamics Among Elements			
IV. Resource Studies			
V. Information Systems			

influence existing in the field of training in community mental health.

—To determine the general philosophies and directives emanating from these components.

—To derive second-order objectives related to these general philosophies and directives.

—To devise measures and reporting systems necessary to determine progress toward these objectives.

—To feed back this information to various levels of decisionmaking.

II. General Structure of Training in Community Mental Health: A Sample of Structural Elements and their Presumed Philosophical Dedications

    A. Federal Government

       1. Elected Officials

          To translate the intent of the electorate into administrative realities.

          —To support an educational system that will provide mental health services.

          ... That will provide control over socially disruptive persons who are mentally ill.

          ... That will provide timely and effective care for such persons.

          ... That will provide services that are not too costly—to the taxpayer, to community functioning, to the patients.

          ... That will attack and reduce mental illness and related social problems that are believed to be of high priority.

2. Appointees: HEW, NIMH
   —To respond to the above by sponsoring training programs and research.
   —To devise programs and allocate resources that are responsible to current dedication and leadership of professional organizations.
   —To add to current state of knowledge in the areas of mental health, community mental health, education, etc.

B. Education
   Medical schools
   Graduate schools
   Professional training schools—allied health professions

C. Professional Organizations
   AMA, APA, APAP, ACSW, etc.

D. General Public
   Articulate majority and minority groups

The structural outline would proceed in this manner, identifying the major sources of input into the training system and listing the formal and informal dedications. If one were to actually carry out this process, one would attempt to establish a weighting system between elements and within elements. This could take the form of a regression equation or some other mathematical model or some variant of our goal-scaling model. In this way one would be forming a transition to the next stage of the evaluation: a description of the dynamics.

III. Dynamics

As one takes the elements listed in structure, an effort should be made to specify functional relationships among them. The terms employed would be something like:

Determines all policy for

Determines some (specify) policy for

Policy influenced (specify degree) by information from

Provides resources for (specify percent and what kind)

This can be diagrammed throughout the system.

IV. Resource Study

A. Resource Flow Study

Resource study would be closely related to the study of the system dynamics. One way of tracing functional relationships would be to follow the funds. Reviews of what happened to community mental health funds are a narrative form of this. A diagram showing the sources of their budget would also imply the degree of control one structural element has over the other.

B. Resource Availability

Another resource study would indicate the total resources — money and manpower — available for the training in community mental health. Money set aside for this topic can be indicated along with time-and-effort studies. The latter can be obtained from existing estimates made by medical schools. The total resources already existing and available for management (direct and indirect) would be important in itself.

C. Resource Allocation

Part of the resource study should include a projected allocation of funds into various cost centers. Among these centers would be several for various kinds of training-related activities, administration, and — important for this committee — evaluation. Knowing the financial commitment, one can estimate the degree of actual commitment to various objectives and activities.

V. The Information System

A. Information System Dynamics (Table 2.2 presents the components of the information system, and feedback loops within it.)

B. Information Collection Loci: An Example Related to a Particular Training Program

Table 2.2

Determine impact of information 8	1	Statement of general intent of dedication
Review #1 and #2 7	2	Determination of objectives related to #1
Feedback information from #5 to decisionmakers 6	3	Determination of measures necessary to #2
Determine outcome of #4 5	4	Monitor the activity

Table 2.3

Locus of Data Collection	Aspect to be Evaluated			
	Students	Faculty	Curriculum	Program Units
University				Total University
Practicum				Total Practicum
Postgraduate Service Center				Total Service Center
	All Students	All Faculty	All Curriculum	Total Program

Table 2.4
INFORMATION REPORTING

User of Information	Type of Information			
	Curriculum Content	Student Performance	Postgraduate Performance	etc.
General Public				
Federal Legislators				
Federal Executive				
Federal Administration				
Professional Organizations				
Graduate and Medical Schools				
Training Departments				
Faculty				
Students				
Clients				
Service Delivery Agencies				
etc.				

Throughout this process of definition and specification one would relate to the levels shown in Table 2.1. Some goals and objectives may be general across the levels, others specific to only some levels or areas within a level. An example might be the goal of producing a certain number of a particular variety of mental health worker. Level I would contain a total manpower dedication, Level II only those portions of the manpower within their capability to produce, Level III a certain number of graduates from a particular program.

The same process would hold for the reporting of the information system. Obviously only some management and outcome information would be reported to the various elements in the structure. A student's satisfaction with a particular curriculum would be information fed to the faculty supervisor; aggregates of student opinion, to faculty committees; total student satisfaction would be only one item in the reporting on the total program to Level II. Level I may receive only a phrase regarding this issue. An information-and-user diagram could be constructed to summarize the reporting.

Part II

How to Do It

An evaluation paradigm, useful in determining the practical aspects of "How to do it," is presented in this section. The tremendous variety of circumstances, programs and goals is taken into account, and two different methods of quantifying and objectifying the values of participants in the training process are offered.

In the past, evaluation researchers have paid little attention to the question of quantification of values, which is, in fact, one of the most important aspects of the evaluation of training process. The two methods presented in this section are well developed and can be put to immediate use in the evaluation-research process.

In each method the values and goals serve as the structure, or basic core, around which the entire evaluation is conducted. Such a structure naturally raises the question, Why this emphasis on methods of evaluation that make these values explicit and give them so important a role in the entire evaluation? This emphasis is derived from the task force focus on (1) making the evaluation of training relevant, and (2) the importance of the underlying values of the programs in understanding program outcomes. Past evaluation methods have emphasized *only* the objective measurement of external processes and outcomes. Although the task force believes in these methods as well, it does emphasize the addition of methods which can make hidden values explicit. The use of such methods makes it possible to link evaluation of training directly to the values of decisionmakers and the actual (though often unspoken) goals of the training.

3

Paradigm for Evaluation of
Training Programs for Community Mental Health

MADELYNN OGLESBY

The federal output for training in mental health in 1967 alone was close to $100 million. Mental health professionals currently employed throughout the United States include 23,000 psychiatrists, 28,000 psychologists, 27,000 nurses and 7,500 social workers (Fagin, 1971).

Caro (1971) cites the "dissatisfaction with the current state of intervention on problems of health, economic security, education and housing." He observes that "increased expenditures have not appreciably improved the social order." He recommends "adequate assessment of existing and innovative programs . . . [as] a vital force in directing social change and improving the lives and the environments of community members."

Suchman (1967) emphasizes increasing pressure for more systematic evaluation of programs as a function of changes in the attitudes of the public toward health needs and services, public demand for scientific proof of effectiveness and changes in the structure and function of public agencies emphasizing broader community participation.

The role of the professional in community mental health centers has been challenged by the paraprofessionals and lay workers employed in the center and by clients receiving care from the system. The major critique of mental health professionals by these people centers on the irrelevance of their practice relative to the crying needs of the community. Admittedly, mental health professionals, trained within the context of the medical model which focuses on treatment of mental illness, have been reluctant to change the foci of their practice from treatment of mental illness to treatment and prevention of community mental health problems such as drug abuse and addiction, high school dropout rates and high delinquency rates. In recognition of the dilemma experienced jointly by mental health professionals and community mental health centers (i.e., the conflict between the mental health needs of the community and the treatment modality of the professional), efforts are continually being made to define content essential to community mental health practice, to include this content and corollary practice in basic programs preparing professionals and to provide continuing and in-service education for practicing community mental health professionals.

Comprehensive evaluation of these programs to determine their quality and their effectiveness is essential if training programs are to be relevant to the actual practice of the community mental health professional and if professional mental health practice is to successfully perform its role in community health centers: i.e., to provide the services which can be rendered only by an individual who has a solid background in the understanding of the dynamics of individual, group, organizational and community dynamics; the process appropriate to the modification of behaviors of each of these components; and the skill in using and assisting paraprofessionals and lay workers to use these processes within the limits of the knowledge and experience of each individual. Evaluation of these programs must take into account the program and the trainee, and must be concerned not only with validating the effectiveness of the program (in relation to the ability of the mental health professional to function in appropriate indirect and direct care roles in the community), but must also be concerned with the need to modify the programs as a result of current measures of effectiveness of the program and long-term changes in the practice of the given profession.

To date, comprehensive evaluation of programs preparing professional practitioners in community mental health has not consistently occurred in all professional programs. Where evaluation does occur it may be piecemeal, focusing only on the program itself (the stated objectives of the program or the teaching-learning methods employed); the trainee (the amount of knowledge he has obtained, the position he has accepted after completion of his program, his attitudes, his opinions, his performance); on the trainer (his qualifications, capacities, experience); and (rarely) on the effect of his practice on the clients he serves (the actual outcome of his practice).

The purpose of this paper is to discuss evaluation of the four types of community mental health training programs for the four professions traditionally involved in providing services in community mental health centers: nursing, medicine, psychology, and social work (Arnhoff et al., 1969). Table 3.1 presents definitions of each of the four types of programs discussed in this paper.

Table 3.1
DEFINITION OF PROGRAMS DISCUSSED IN THIS BOOK

Type	Description	Usual Purpose
A. Basic professional education	Academic program offering a degree (B.S., M.D., M.P.H., Ph.D., etc.)	Preparation of professional to function at a generalist or specialist level in community mental health
B. Postgraduate training in community mental health	Program offered by an institution certified to provide advanced training in community mental health (residency training programs in medicine, post-doctoral training)	Specialization education for the professional in community mental health
C. Continuing education programs in community	Program offered to practicing professionals sponsored by universities, professional organizations and teaching agencies (workshops, symposia, seminars, etc.)	Updating and improvement of community health practice of practicing professionals
D. In-service education programs	Program sponsored by an agency employing mental health professionals	Orientation and improvement of the specific community mental health practice provided by professionals in the agency

The Purposes of Evaluation of Educational Programs

Various purposes for evaluation of educational programs in general can be identified from a sampling of the literature. These purposes can be extrapolated to purposes of evaluation of programs training community mental health professionals. Table 3.2 lists these purposes and attempts to relate each purpose to each of the four types of programs training community mental health professionals.

The listing of purposes in Table 3.2 stops short of a complete list of prescribed purposes of evaluation of programs training mental health professionals to community practice—to determine the effectiveness of the training programs upon the mental health of the community served by the professional. The purposes of evaluation of programs training community mental health professionals are numerous and can be summarized into three broad general purposes: to evaluate the effectiveness of the program; to evaluate the performance of the student and the quality of his practice; and to evaluate the effect of his practice on the clients he serves following the completion of the program. The focus of this paper will be on evaluation of programs through evaluation of the three general purposes specified above.

Evaluation and Evaluative Research

Evaluation of programs training community mental health professionals varies with respect to the degree of scientific rigor required and the uses of their

Table 3.2
PURPOSES OF EVALUATION OF EDUCATIONAL PROGRAMS AND THE RELEVANCE
OF THESE PURPOSES TO THE FOUR TYPES OF PROGRAMS TRAINING
Community Mental Health Professionals

Purposes Defined by Literature	Basic	Postgraduate	Continuing Education	In-Service
I. Purposes as related to students				
A. To judge performance (Cronbach, 1963)	X	X	X	X
B. To determine motivation of student (Dressel and Mayhew, 1954; Rines, 1963)	X	X		
C. To determine student progress (Rines, 1963)	X	X		
D. To help the individual student maintain strengths and eliminate weaknesses (Rines, 1963)	X	X	X	X
E. To provide psychological support for the student, staff and community (Rines, 1963)	X	X	X	X
F. To provide certification to meet legal requirements (Rines, 1963)	X	X		
II. Purposes as related to programs				
A. To improve a course or program (Cronbach, 1963, 1964)	X	X	X	X
B. To investigate program effectiveness (Dressel and Mayhew, 1954)	X	X	X	X
C. To determine the value of a course (Rines, 1963)	X	X	X	
D. To clarify and refine educational objectives (Rines, 1963)	X	X	X	X
E. To determine how well the program objectives are being met (Bigman)	X	X	X	X
F. To specify objectives in terms of outcomes (Freeman and Sherwood, 1971)	X	X	X	X
G. To determine costs more realistically (Freeman and Sherwood, 1971)		X		X
III. Purposes as related to processes or components of the program				
A. To improve teaching (Rines, 1963)	X	X	X	X
B. To identify reasons for specific successes and failures (Bigman)	X	X	X	X
C. To identify the principles underlying a successful program (Bigman)	X	X	X	X
D. To identify effective techniques (Bigman)	X	X	X	X
E. To identify alternative successful methods for attaining goals (Freeman and Sherwood, 1971)	X	X		
IV. Purposes as related to evaluation procedures				
A. To develop more reliable instruments for evaluation (Rines, 1963)	X	X		
V. Purposes as related to recipients of services to students				
A. To provide certification to meet legal requirements (Rines, 1963)	X	X		

results. As results of the evaluation are used, the degree of scientific rigor must be clearly defined to avoid misinterpretation of scientifically derived facts or, conversely, to avoid misinterpretation of unsystematically obtained impressions. Suchman makes a distinction between evaluation and evaluative research. The former is a judgment of the value of a program, while the latter is the more formal scientific systematic use of research procedures for evaluating a program. Each type of evaluation is appropriate for some uses, and neither should be discounted as useless. However, both evaluation and evaluative research should be used in appropriate situations with appropriate interpretation and utilization of results (Suchman, 1967, p. 22). Throughout the remainder of this paper, Suchman's definitions of the terms *evaluation* and *evaluative research* will be used. The term *assessment* will be used to refer to both evaluation and evaluative research.

Evaluation

Stake (1967, 523–24) describes informal evaluation, based on casual observation, implicit goals, intuitive norms and subjective judgment which may be "penetrating and insightful" or "superficial and distorted." This type of evaluation is used traditionally (both appropriately and inappropriately) by people such as legislators, administrators, practitioners, recipients of services and journalists (Caro, 1971).

Suchman (1967) defines evaluation as "the social process of making value judgments of worth . . . the general process of appraisal" and identifies six different abuses of evaluation: (1) eyewash, where an attempt is made to justify a program by deliberately selecting only those aspects which look good; (2) whitewash, where an attempt is made to cover up program failures or errors by appraisals such as testimonials; (3) submarine, where the intent is to destroy a program regardless of its worth; (4) posture, where evaluation is used as a gesture of objectivity and a pose of scientific research; (5) postponement, where there is an attempt to delay the needed action by pretending to seek facts; and (6) substitution, where an attempt is made to disguise failures of an essential part of the program by shifting attention to some less relevant but more defensible aspect of the program.

The validity of evaluation is determined by (1) the evaluator and (2) the information he uses for his evaluation.

The evaluator may bias his evaluation either for or against the particular program because of a vested interest in, or a particular antipathy toward, a program component or program. Campbell suggests that administrators and politicians oftentimes give very positive evaluations of their pet programs or projects and resist any attempt to verify this evaluation with systematic and scientific methods. The educational and experiential background of the evaluator will also determine, to some extent, the validity of his evaluation. Presumably, the more knowledgeable about a given type of program, the more accurate his evaluation.

The evaluator's familiarity with the program may also influence his evaluation. If he is an outsider he may miss certain valuable implicit aspects of the program, while if he is an insider he may see value in some aspects of the program which do not really exist. Caro (1971) discusses the advantages of outside versus inside evaluators. Outsiders are better able to maintain objectivity; more likely to include evaluative criteria which question the basic organizational premises; more likely and able to mediate internal conflicts; usually protected from the marginality and status incongruity often encountered by insiders; and better able to avoid unwelcome research tasks. Inside evaluators are able to develop detailed knowledge into the organization and its programs and are in a better position to do continuing research.

TYPES OF EVALUATION

Four types of evaluation can be defined on the basis of the information and criteria used for the evaluation. The information varies with respect to the manner in which it was collected, and the criteria varies with respect to its visibility to others.

Impressionistic evaluations are the least factual and valid of the four types of evaluation. The evaluator usually collects information about a program through chance. No attempt is made to verify if these chance observations are accurate and a representative sample of what usually occurs. The criteria for impressionistic evaluation are vague and generally unstated. Validity of this evaluation is questionable unless the observational ability of the evaluator is high, he has an unbiased sample of observations and he possesses sufficient knowledge and experience to apply appropriate criteria to evaluating his observations.

Opinionistic evaluations are estimations of the value of a given program or program component which are based on systematic observation of the actual program (or reporting of the program by someone knowledgeable about the program) as compared with a stated or unstated ideal situation. Generally, experts in the field are asked to give an opinionistic evaluation of programs or components. However, the evaluation is only as good as the information provided the evaluator (through direct observation or reporting of others), the evaluator's expertness in the field, the sampling procedure used for observations and the ideal situation being used by the evaluator to develop his opinion of the value of the program.

Judgmental evaluations are based on systematic and representative observations of the program and a predetermined and clearly defined set of criteria. Evaluation of a program or program component using judgments is valid if the observations are made accurately and reliably, if they are a representative sample of what usually goes on and if the predetermined set of criteria is valid for the particular evaluation and such evaluations in general.

Factual evaluations are based on empirical data obtained from actual events without the need for observation, interpretation or valuation by a second person. Facts are obtained by making direct observations of the presence or absence of a thing, and by asking respondents, who possess the information about themselves or their part in the program, to report them through paper-and-pencil tests, through interviews, etc. The validity of facts is determined by the observational skill of the observer, the honesty of the respondent, his ability to give honest answers without fear of retribution and his ability to report such information through whatever format is being used to collect the facts. In obtaining facts from a sample of a larger population, the validity of the facts is determined by the representativeness of the sample used for the entire population. If the sample is not representative of the entire population, then the facts obtained from the sample are valid only for the sample and not for the entire population.

FACTORS WHICH INFLUENCE EVALUATION

Factors, in addition to those already mentioned which influence any of the four types of evaluation of any program, include the purpose of the evaluation, the duration of the evaluation and the attitude of the evaluatees toward the evaluator, the evaluation process and the program.

Often evaluation is done for the purpose of granting or withholding support funds to, or accreditation or approval of, a proposed or ongoing program. The administrators, teachers and participants of the program will invariably try to impress the evaluator with the value of the program in an effort to receive continued support or accreditation of the program. In this situation it is unlikely that evaluation of the program will uncover any major flaws if they can possibly be hidden from the evaluators. On the other hand, evaluators, whose purpose is to improve the program, may diligently seek out flaws to the extent that some positive aspects of the program may be omitted or modified because they were identified in some part of the program as "less than perfect."

The duration and time of the evaluation process is also an influencing factor in the value of any program evaluation. The evaluator must have spent enough time with the program to have an idea of what is usually being done in the program. An outside evaluator who comes in for two days to observe the program and whose intent and purpose (i.e., that he is evaluating the program) is known to participants in the program, is likely to observe not the usual, but some permutation of the usual which has occurred as the function of his presence (Hawthorne effect) over a short period of time. This effect may occur even if his purpose is not known. Given a longer period of observation, the participants are less likely to be able to maintain the unusual behavior and are also more likely to become accustomed to his presence. It is also questionable whether an evaluator can make all observations necessary for a "true" evaluation within a limited span of time.

Procedures for selecting observation time will influence the validity of the evaluation. Ideally, observations should be randomly selected over a sufficient period of time to insure that adequate information is available for a valid evaluation. This is not always possible. Evaluation based on a biased sample of observations should be avoided at all costs and some procedure should be defined for ensuring that adequate observational samples are made of all components of the program.

The attitudes of the evaluatees of the program toward evaluation, the evaluator and the program itself may bias the observation. If the evaluatees are threatened by the evaluation or the evaluator, they will be less likely to communicate negative aspects of the program. If one of the evaluatees has a vested interest in some component of the program, he may attempt to focus the evaluator's attention to the merits of that program and simultaneously focus attention away from the program flaws. Evaluatees have also been known to produce invalid negative observations for an evaluator who objects to the program or would like to see it closed.

In summary, evaluation of programs preparing mental health professionals to practice in the community contain certain possible "invalidating" elements. If the type of evaluation is indicated (i.e., impressionistic, opinionistic, judgmental or factual), if the procedures for evaluation assure unbiased observations of the true characteristics of the program and if the evaluator and evaluatees are both oriented to the necesssity for a "true" evaluation, the evaluation will more than likely be a true estimate of what is actually being done in and by the program.

Evaluative Research

In the past few years a body of literature has emerged which suggests the application of traditional research methods to the assessment of social and health programs. Assessment, including evaluative research, is a major component of systematic program development and is used for identification of problems, specification of objectives, analysis of the causes of the problems and an examination of shortcomings of existing programs (Caro, 1971).

A majority of methods focus on the assessment of the ability of the program to carry out its stated goals. Some tend to focus more on what goes into the program relative to planning—what sorts of information are used for planning the program—while others focus on the output of the program—what is the effect of the program on the target populations it serves (Caro, 1971).

Both of these foci are relevant to the assessment of educational programs preparing mental health professionals in the community. Assessments of input lend themselves to evaluation, as opposed to evaluative research, while assessments of output lend themselves to evaluative research.

This section of the paper is devoted to a discussion of evaluative research as described by Suchman (1967), Caro (1971), Campbell (1969, 1971) and others. The evaluative research model is roughly comparable to the operations research and action research methods described by Cherns (1971), the goal-attainment model of Schulberg, Sheldon, and Baker (1969), the evaluative or programmatic model described by Hyman (Suchman, 1967, pp. 75–76), and the program-testing method described by Hovland (Suchman, 1967, p. 77).

Evaluative research is "the utilization of scientific research methods and techniques for the purpose of making an evaluation" (Suchman, 1967, p. 7). Its "primary goal is not the discovery of new knowledge but a testing of the application of knowledge" in planning. Its major utility is to determine if a given program or procedure is achieving the desired results. Hypotheses tested in the research are derived from the stated objectives and procedures of the program and operation of programs (Suchman, 1967, p. 75). It provides the basic information for designing and redesigning action programs . . . aims at increased understanding of applied or administrative processes . . . and involves more than judging; it also encompasses understanding and redefinition" (Suchman, 1967, pp. 30–31). It utilizes "these procedures for collecting and analyzing data which increase the probability of 'proving' rather than assessing the worth of some social activity" (Suchman, 1967, pp. 7–8). Evaluative research is costly and requires that trained research personnel be employed to evaluate a given program.

In evaluative research the designs are essentially the same as for other quasiexperimental or experimental studies. Campbell (1969) speaks, in detail, about the use of designs for social experiments. His coverage includes three preexperimental designs (the one-shot case study, the one-group pre- and post-test design and the static group comparison) and four true experimental designs (pre-post test control group, Solomon four-group design, post-test-only control-group design and multiple treatment designs). He elucidates the limitations of each design in detail.

Suchman discusses the need in evaluative research design for the entire program to be flexible so that hypotheses, identified after the implementation of the design, can also be tested. The flexibility also allows for implementation and testing of needed modifications in the program, identified within the context of the research. Suchman warns, however, that when flexibility interferes with scientific rigor, the flexibility must be sacrificed in the interests of scientific rigor (1967).

Herzog (1969) describes a series of questions to be asked when planning evaluative research: (1) the purpose of evaluation; (2) the change desired; (3) the methods to be used for assessing the change including reliability and validity of categories and measures, the time intervals for measurement, the representativeness of the sample and the control of extraneous and intervening variables; (4) the findings. She identifies three types of evaluative research: ultimate evaluation, which tests effects with global measures; preevaluative research, which includes studies of specific effects contributing to the ultimate evaluation; and short-term evaluation, which is accomplished within a few years. Suchman identifies three main conditions of evaluative research: (1) sampling of equivalent experimental and control groups; (2) isolation and control of the stimulus (the independent variable); and (3) definition of the response (dependent variable) (1967, 102–208). The measurement of effects of programs also requires the specification of four major categories of variables: (1) component parts or processes of the program; (2) specific population or target group reached; (3) situational conditions within which the program occurs; and (4) differential effects of the program (Suchman, 1967, p. 115).

PROBLEMS IN EVALUATIVE RESEARCH

Caro (1971) identifies some problems encountered in conducting evaluative research. It requires cooperation from agency administrators, the researcher may experience status ambiguities, the practitioners may be reluctant to collect the data and publication may be inhibited.

Mann (1971) speaks of some of the technical difficulties in using research designs such as the pre-post control group design. Among these problems are the reliability, appropriateness and independence of the tools used to measure changes; the confounding of change effects by competing extraneous variables such as the personalities of the practitioner, changing environments and the degree of expertness of the practitioner in his practice or in certain areas of his practice; the Hawthorne effect; control of contamination of the control group; and control of the experimental group.

The problems in conducting evaluative research in social and health programs are no different from those encountered in any research design with human subjects. Control of variables is a major problem in any applied research procedure. However, research methodology literature suggests a number of procedures for such problems. None of them are entirely failproof. However, with some caution and care on the part of the researcher, some of the limitations of evaluated experimentation in programs can be overcome. Uncontrolled limitations must be identified clearly and their potential influence on the outcome of the study must be made explicit in planning and conducting the study.

In the assessment of programs preparing mental health professionals to practice in the community, a combination of evaluation and systematic evaluative research can be employed to develop maximum information about the program itself and its value to the trainees and the clients served by the trainees of the program. Various elements or foci being evaluated may be more amenable to either evaluation or evaluative research. Additionally, the type of program (basic professional, postgraduate, continuing education and in-service) and the purpose of the evaluation will also determine, to some extent, the use and type of evaluation and evaluative research appropriate in the assessment of a given program or program component. Table 3.3 defines the various evaluation and evaluative research strategies which can be used for evaluation on the four types of educational programs being discussed in this paper. Table 3.3 also includes the sources of data for each type of evaluation for each type of program and suggests experimental designs to be used in evaluative research.

FOCI FOR ASSESSMENT OF PROGRAMS

Numerous foci for assessment of educational programs have been identified. These are summarized in Table 3.4.

Three major targets of assessment are derived from the list of foci: the trainee, the program, and the recipient of practice. Comprehensive assessment of a program training the community mental health professional would include each of these targets. However, emphasis on various targets of assessment varies somewhat with the type of program. For example, emphasis may be placed on the trainee and the program in Type A program (basic professional programs),

Table 3.3
A SUGGESTED WAY TO USE EVALUATION AND EVALUATIVE RESEARCH
APPLIED TO THE EVALUATION OF THE FOUR TYPES OF PROGRAMS

Type of Program	Evaluation				Evaluative Research
	Impressions	Opinions	Judgments	Facts	
Basic Professional Programs	Students, employers, recipients of services	Students, employers, recipients of services	Students, employers	Employers Recipients of services	One-shot case study Comparison of performance of group receiving professional training with a second group receiving no such training; or comparison of two groups receiving different types of training in the same profession One group pre- and post- design
Postgraduate	Same as above	Same as above	Same as above	Same as above	Same as above
Continuing Education	Same as above	Same as above	Same as above	Same as above	Same as above plus Pre-post control-group design comparing performance of trainees with performance of a comparable group of professionals with no such training Multiple treatment designs
In-Service	Same as above	Same as above	Same as above	Same as above	Same as above

while in Type D programs (in-service programs), emphasis may be on assessment of the program through the effect of a given professional practitioner (an in-service trainee) upon clients served by the agency.

Figure 3.1 portrays an overall plan for comprehensive assessment of training community mental health professionals. Reading from left to right, five foci of assessment have been identified: (1) factors determining the content and process of the program; (2) the program itself; (3) the trainee in the program; (4) trainee practice after completion of the program; and (5) the clients who are recipients of direct or indirect practice by the professional.

The paradigm is intended to represent compo-

Table 3.4
FOCI FOR EVALUATION OF TRAINING PROGRAMS[a]

I. Trainees

    Opinions
    Attitudes
    Achievement
        Knowledge of facts and/or principles
        Behavior logically related to outcome
            Simulated experiences
            Real-life experiences
    Changes in job performances
        Personal effectiveness
        Tangible products
        Specific behavioral elements
        Gross performance
        Inferred performance
        Malperformance

II. Program

    Determination of trainee needs
    Participant motivation and interest
    Objectives
    Curricula procedures
        Course of study
        Learning-teaching principles
        Instruction
        Lesson plans
        Instructional materials
        Training aids and equipment
        Examination
    Instructor qualifications

III. Client

    Effect on client
    Type of client

[a]Compiled from references

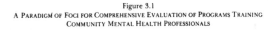

Figure 3.1
A PARADIGM OF FOCI FOR COMPREHENSIVE EVALUATION OF PROGRAMS TRAINING
COMMUNITY MENTAL HEALTH PROFESSIONALS

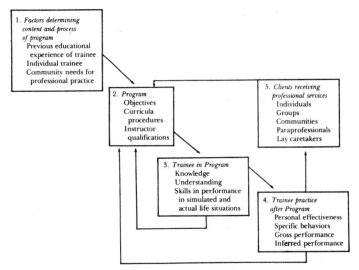

nents or foci of the assessment from the initiation of a program (step 1) to the final outcome of the program as demonstrated by effects on the clients (step 5). It is also intended to indicate feedback points into the program for its modification based on the results of evaluative research.

The targets of a comprehensive assessment of training programs portrayed in Figure 3.1 are useful in defining some sample questions for evaluating programs training mental health professionals and in identifying various assessment methods which can be used to answer these questions. These assessment methods include the four types of evaluation identified previously in this paper where more rigorous methods are not possible, and the more controlled and systematic evaluative research methods which depend upon valid, reliable, quantified data and scientific design.

Factors Determining Content and Process of the Program

Three factors are identified as major determinants in the content and process of the program: previous educational experiences of trainees, community needs for professional practice and individual trainee needs. Some training programs are susceptible to such factors, while others may be influenced minimally. In-service programs probably depend heavily upon the individual trainee and community needs as determining factors in any program, continuing education programs generally rely on individual trainee needs, while academic and postgraduate programs are less susceptible to short-term changes in these two factors. Assessment of programs may examine the influence and the relevance of each of these factors in determining the content and process of the program. A number of techniques have been developed for determination of training needs. Some of these techniques are listed in Table 3.5.

Some sample questions for assessment of this first focus follow. Each question is succeeded by a classification of evaluation and evaluative research methods useful in answering that question:

What methods were used to identify *individual trainee needs* (e.g., survey of trainee using questionnaire, interview, checklist)? *Factual evaluation.* How were the results used in planning the program?

Table 3.5
TECHNIQUES AND FOCI FOR DETERMINING TRAINING NEEDS [b]

Techniques	Types of data
Job Analysis	Weekly work schedules
Checklist surveys	Resume of patient contacts over a period of time
Interviews	Listing of diagnostic entities,
Observations	problems resolved and unresolved
Performance appraisals	Personnel changes
Opinions surveys	Personnel statistics

[b]Compiled from references

Factual, judgmental, opinionistic and *impressionistic evaluation.*

What methods were used to identify *community needs* for professional mental health practice not currently available? *Factual evaluation.* Were these methods appropriate? *Opinionistic and impressionistic.* Were community needs adequately sampled and by whom? *Judgmental, opinionistic and impressionistic evaluation.* How were the results used in planning the training program for the professional? *Factual evaluation.*

Were community and trainee needs consistent? If not, which set of needs determined the thrust of the program? *Factual and opinionistic evaluation.*

Strategies for assessing programs for the use of information generated about trainee needs and community needs for additional professional mental health practice rest, to a large extent, upon evaluation as compared with evaluative research.

In planning programs, the use of information about needs of individual trainees varies with respect to the type of program. In academic and postgraduate programs solicitation of individual trainee needs over the years with continuous development and modification of a "profile of trainees" (norms) is probably the appropriate strategy. In continuing education programs individual trainee needs should be taken into account when planning programs. In in-service programs, where emphasis is on the specific practice of specific individuals, individual trainee needs should be sampled in detail and should be directly used in the planning of the program. In general, the more factual and complete the information about the trainee needs, the better the program.

The same holds true for the use of community needs for additional or improved professional mental health practice. Usually, academic and postgraduate programs are based on a composite of community needs for professional practice (a "norm" community developed from numerous courses including the literature, surveys of the communities where former trainees are practicing, etc.), while in-service education programs are more concerned with the identified needs of an actual and specific community. In the latter case, if "trainee needs" seem to be in conflict with community needs, community needs should assume precedence over trainee needs. For example, if the trainees appear to need additional training in individual psychotherapy while the community need is for professional services in the treatment and prevention of drug abuse (and the trainees are not able, without additional training, to perform such service), then emphasis should be placed upon training to serve the community needs.

Program Components

Components of program include: objectives, curricula procedures and instructor qualifications. Each of these components will be discussed separately.

PROGRAM OBJECTIVES

Specification of objectives is a prerequisite for assessment (Miller, 1964). Stake (1968) emphasizes the need for central objectives designed to define the thrust of the program. Programs can be assessed on the basis of (1) presence of training objectives; (2) clarity of objectives; (3) relevancy of the objectives for the type of training program and the needs of the trainee; and (4) relevancy of the objectives to the needs of the community where the client will be practicing.

CURRICULA PROCEDURES

Include the course of study, learning-teaching principles, instruction, lesson plans, instructional materials, training aids and equipment and methods of evaluation. Assessment of programs can focus on the presence of identified content, teaching methods and qualified instructors and their relevance to the stated objectives, the needs and the background of the trainees and the needs of the community where the trainee will be practicing.

Questions are listed below which may be asked relative to the program curricula:

1. Are the objectives stated clearly and concisely and do they indicate the terminal behavior expected of trainees? *Factual evaluation*.
2. Are the objectives relevant to the trainee and community needs? *Factual, judgmental, opinionistic evaluation*.
3. Can the objectives be tested—i.e., can trainee behavior resulting from the program be observed and quantified? *Factual, judgmental evaluation*.
4. Are the curricula procedures (i.e., content, teaching methods, etc.) appropriate, relative to the needs of the trainee and his level of understanding and to the community needs? *Judgmental, opinionistic, impressionistic evaluation*.
5. Are the curricula procedures appropriate to the stated objectives of the program? *Judgmental, opinionistic, impressionistic evaluation*.
6. Are teaching methods consistent with the principles of adult learning? *Judgmental, opinionisitc, impressionistic evaluation*.
7. Are instructional personnel qualified? *Factual evaluation*. Have they engaged in professional community mental health *practice? Factual evaluation*. Do they have an appropriate educational background? *Judgmental, opinionistic evaluation*.

These questions about the program assess whether the program, as planned is: clearly defined (question 1); testable (question 3); relevant (question

2); logically consistent (question 5); appropriate to the trainee (question 6); and taught by clinically and educationally prepared staff (question 7).

Questions 1 and 3 also provide criteria for a more systematic testing of the effects of the program on the trainee. Suchman (1967) speaks of objectives of programs, if stated clearly and concisely, as being overall hypotheses for testing of the program. In this instance, the objectives can be used as hypotheses of the effect of the program on trainees.

The literature suggests some more specific foci for assessment. De Long (1967) emphasizes the need for a definition of specific goals and attention to individual requirements in trainee programs, while Miller (1964) suggests that the student must have a clear picture of the behavior he is to adopt. Enelow and Adler (1965) suggest the necessity for carefully defined objectives, carefully designed course methods (e.g., live presentations and discussions, observation through a one-way mirror, supervised clinical courses), and the careful attention to the training of instructors and the maintenance of student motivation when planning postgraduate courses in psychiatry. Gagne (1965) identifies, among components of the instructional situation, the provision of a model for terminal performance and the assessment of learning attainments. Cassels (1961) lists eight steps to better training in adults. The eight steps can be condensed to four: the adult must be motivated to learn, he must have an opportunity to use what he learns in practice; his learning centers on problems; he learns best in an informal environment; and his experience affects his learning.

Content in programs to prepare professional

mental health practitioners is emerging. Fergerson (1966) discusses the content of community health programs: community service; organizational theory and behavior; and public health concepts and principles, including prevention, epidemiology, community organization, administration, rehabilitation, consultation, social welfare and positive mental health. He points out the need for a flexible posture for all professionals. Hume (1964) emphasizes the need for the professional to accept new responsibilities as the relationships among professional roles change. Hodges (1964) suggests that the professional's role in the community is that of a facilitator, as contrasted with a manipulator. The professional must have a high degree of confidence in the community's capacity to grow, learn and repair its own insufficiencies. Kelly (1966, *1970*) has suggested the ecological framework for community psychology practice, while Halpert (*1970*) suggests the systems approach to the delivery of mental health services.

Trainees in the Program

Trainee performance during the program is another item which can be used to assess the programs. Trainee performance includes such things as the possession of knowledge of facts and principles presented in the program (measured by paper-and-pencil tests) and the behavior utilizing this knowledge in practice (simulated and real-life experience), which can be measured by rating scales and the like. Trainee performance as measured by the above techniques can be compared with the stated program objectives to determine the adequacy of the curricula procedures in achieving the objectives.

Questions which may be asked of the program to trainee performance include the following:

1. Does the trainee possess sufficient knowledge and understanding of the content being presented? *Factual, judgmental, opinionistic and impressionistic evaluation.*
2. Is the amount of knowledge and understanding possessed by the trainee during, and at the end of, the training sufficiently greater than before the training program began? *One-group pre-post evaluative research.*
3. Is the trainee able to use his knowledge and understanding in simulated or real-life experiences? *Factual, judgmental, opinionistic and impressionistic evaluation.*
4. Is his performance in simulated and real-life situations appreciably improved at the end of the training program when compared to the beginning of the program? *One-group pre-post evaluative research.*
5. Can the trainee perform, to criterion, those behaviors being modified by the training program? *Evaluation of all four types.*
6. How many of the trainees successfully completed the program to criterion? *Factual evaluation.*

These questions introduce the possibility of more precise measures of the effect of the program as it is related to the trainee's behavior. Quantitative data can be generated about trainees by the use of paper-and-pencil tests, rating scales, questionnaires, etc. With the availability of quantitative data, hypotheses can be tested and a systematic evaluation of programs using empirical data and evaluative research designs can be accomplished. Such questions presume clearly stated objectives which identify the anticipated behavioral changes in the trainee at the termination of the program.

The questions readily suggest a pre-post test one-group design for assessment of the effect of training on the trainee. The addition of a control group whose members have not received such training, would provide contrast information for evaluation of the effect of the training on the trainee.

Trainee Practice After Program

The program can also be assessed through the job performance of the trainee at intervals after the completion of the program. Figure 3.1 lists four possible components of trainee performance which can be evaluated. In addition, comparisons of pre- and post-training job performance of the trainee, comparisons of in-training and post-training performance and comparison of post-training with the stated program objectives, provide systematic evaluation of the program effects on the trainee.

Sample questions which lend themselves to evaluative research designs are listed below:

1. Is the trainee significantly more successful in carrying out his responsibilities for which he

has received training after completion of his training. *One-group pre-post evaluative research.*

2. Are trainee behaviors specifically modified by the training program maintained for a significant period of time after the training period? *One-group pre-post evaluative research.*

3. Is the trainee able to apply the knowledge and understanding, gained through training in his practice, following termination of the program? *Factual, opinionistic, impressionistic evaluation.*

4. In general, does the trainee perform efficiently following termination of the program? as compared with his performance before the program? *One-group post evaluative research and one-group pre-post evaluative research.*

5. Are clients (individuals, groups, and communities) satisfied with the professional's performance? *Factual evaluation.*

Assessment of the trainee's performance after the completion of a training program is probably a crucial element in evaluation of training programs in general. This component of assessment may also be more difficult and frustrating, since it rests on the necessity to keep track of the trainees who have completed the program. It may also require that a third party, either employers or recipients of the professional's services, be involved in the assessment. A number of tools can be used to collect information useful in evaluating the trainees' performance: rating scales, self-assessment

by the professional, narrative description, video and
audio tapes of performance and check lists.

All of the questions listed above are appropriate to
assessment of trainees from any of the four types of
programs: academic, postgraduate, continuing education and in-service. Quantified data can be generated
initially, as in the case of direct rating scales and checklists, or converted through content analysis of the narrative descriptions, and video and audio tapes, into
frequency categories. Once quantitative data has been
generated, statistical analysis can be performed which
would test the hypotheses of effects of training programs upon the trainee.

Clients Receiving Professional Service

Perhaps the most crucial component of assessment of training programs for community mental
health professionals is the impact of their practice,
whether it is newly acquired through academic programs or improved through one of the other forms of
training programs. The ultimate purpose of training
programs for professionals is to provide certain and
improved services to those people needing such services. Consequently, the ultimate test of the program is
whether trainees provide improved service to their
clients. Unfortunately, in community mental health
practice, the effects of practice are so confounded by
other factors that it is difficult, if not impossible, to
actually determine effects. However, concerted effort
should be directed to identifying: (1) client behaviors
amenable to change by a given professional; (2) professional behaviors which produce positive change in

the client behaviors; and (3) other variables which may also influence client behaviors being studied as a function of professional practice. "Target" client and practitioner behaviors for evaluating the practice of trainees from professional training programs should be identifiable from program objectives—in a very general form in basic academic and postgraduate programs and in a specific form in in-service programs. (This is another test of the program objectives: do they define client and practitioner behaviors precisely?)

Questions which may be asked about the effectiveness of the practice of the mental health professional are listed below.

1. Do individual clients, groups, or communities receiving professional services from trainees who have completed the program show significantly more improvement (or less deterioration) in certain problems when compared with individual clients, or groups cared for by professionals not exposed to the program? *or* when compared over time (i.e., before the professional received training as compared with after training)? *Pre-post control group evaluative research.*

2. Is there a relationship between the enhanced skill of the professional, as a result of training, and individual client or group improvement in those areas of need for which the professional was specifically trained? *One-group pre-post evaluative research.*

3. Do community needs for which the profes-

sional has been specifically trained show a decrease or decelerated increase after receiving services of a professional who has been trained to meet those needs? *One-group pre-post evaluative research.*

4. Is the paraprofessional more successful in his role after receiving consultation and supervision from a professional who has been trained to meet those needs? *One-group pre-post evaluative research.*

5. Are lay caretakers more successful in their roles after exposure to a professional who has completed a training program? *One-group pre-post evaluative research.*

Questions 1 through 3 are posited for assessment of the trainee's effect on clients receiving professional services from him. This requires that the effects of his services be distinctly identified and measured both before and after and/or compared with a comparable group of "no treatment" clients following the introduction of the professional's practice. Separation of the effect of a given professional's practice from the effects of the practice of other professionals and the enviroment in general is often difficult, if not impossible. Techniques are available for controlling for such confounding variables—e.g., controlled selection of samples and covariance techniques. Assessment of the effect of the services of a specific professional or group of professionals, then, requires that the anticipated effects of practice and any intervening variables are clearly specified and measurable (or can be controlled through sample selection or covariance techniques in the case of the intervening variable).

Questions 4 and 5 relate to the professional's role as consultant, teacher and backup support to the paraprofessional and the lay mental health worker. Assessment of effects of the professional's training upon these two recipients of his services is confounded by the individual and often innate skills of these recipients. Consequently, when assessing effects of the professional practitioner trainee in this realm, control for the innate and learned abilities of the paraprofessional and the lay workers is essential. This is possible through a pre-test of the success of these individuals in their roles before the introduction of a newly trained or retrained professional who provides guidance and supervision to these people.

Briefly, then, to summarize the above discussion, training programs for community mental health professionals can be comprehensively assessed by identifying the key components of the program, asking precise questions about each component and examining its interaction with other components. Various strategies are available for such assessment and range from the impressionistic evaluation to controlled and systematic evaluations using traditional research designs.

Summary

Evaluation of programs preparing professionals for community mental health practices varies with respect to the type of program (basic professional, postgraduate, continuing education and in-service) and the purpose of the evaluation (assessment of student performance, assessment and improvement of program and accreditation). Methods for evaluating programs are classified as evaluation (judgments of the value of the program)and evaluative research, which uses systematic and scientific procedures for assessing programs. Five foci for evaluation can be defined: the use of factors determining content and process of the program in planning the program; the program itself, including content and processes used; the trainee in the program; the trainee following completion of the program; and the effect of the trainee's practice on client mental health needs. The first two foci are more amenable to evaluation, while the latter three lend themselves to evaluative research methods. Evaluation of programs will be determined by the purpose of the evaluation and the intent of the evaluators. Any comprehensive evaluation should include both the subjective and systematic evaluation methods and should consider all five foci for evaluation.

4

Goal-Attainment Scoring
and Quantification of Values

THOMAS KIRESUK

In psychology there are many traditions that could lead one to goal-oriented measurement. Very simply stated, the schools of motivation and dynamic psychology indicate that the human organism is trying to get at something. Knowing what that something is and studying the means by which it is gotten or striven for, constitute central issues for measurement. Level of aspiration studies, for instance, compare actual performance of a subject to his hoped for expectations. The study of achievement motivation also leads to

Partially reprinted from *Evaluation* by permission of the Minneapolis Medical Research Foundation, Inc. Copyright © 1973.

examination of goals and their measurement. McClelland & Winter (1969) developed a measure to determine progress towards a set of goals that are uniquely determined for each subject in his study of the motivation of economic achievement.

In experimental psychology, the work of Skinner (1953) eventually led to the development of behavior therapies in mental health settings. These behavior therapies require careful documentation of current behavior and specification of behavioral change to be achieved by the treatment.

Pollard and Mitchel (1972), in their article on decision theory and power, state that a common theme in a number of areas of psychology is that "behavior is a function of the probability or degree to which behavior leads to various outcomes or consequences and the value or utility of these consequences." Our measure requires setting expected levels of outcome for a unique set of goals. In order to do so, one has to guess what the outcome of training is going to be like. Subjective probability—individual judgment of the likelihood that an outcome will occur as the result of an action—is a major construct in decision theories.

To use the method, one says, "you tell us what you are trying to do and we will help you measure progress towards that event or entity, whatever it is. Use anyone's standards or tests, make up new ones if you like. Choose only those variables that you believe are important for this program or individual. Weight those variables relative to one another any way you like. Pick outcome events that will occur at a future date of your own choosing. Select these outcome events so that they will be indicators of the essential quality you are after, even if you can't state exactly what that quality is. Tailormake these dimensions and outcomes for each program or individual. If they are so truly unique to that patient only, we need never use them again. If common dimensions and outcomes start to occur for particular kinds of patients or settings, we will group them. You can combine commonly used scales or dimensions with unique, used-only-once scales. If you think you know best and have the power to enforce your judgment, just write down your standards as indicated above, and you will find out how well these standards have been met."

Essentially the method has the following characteristics:

1. A set of dimensions devised for or by the individual.
2. A system to assign weights among the dimensions.
3. A set of expected outcomes devised for each dimension.
4. A score summarizing the outcome across all the dimensions.

An illustration of the goal-attainment scoring procedure in clinical work:

Figure 4.1 illustrates a followup guide written by a clinician in a crisis unit. Five scale headings were chosen by the clinician as being important concerns. The titles chosen for the scales would be any words or phrases which would help the followup worker understand the nature of the dimension on which the patient

FIGURE 4.1

Sample Clinical Guide: Crisis Intervention Center

PROGRAM EVALUATION PROJECT

GOAL ATTAINMENT FOLLOW-UP GUIDE

Level at Intake: ✓
Level at Follow-up: *

Level at Intake: 29.4
Goal Attainment Score (Level at Follow-up): 62.2
Goal Attainment Change Score: +32.8

Check whether or not the scale has been mutually negotiated between patient and CIC interviewer.

SCALE ATTAINMENT LEVELS	SCALE 1: Education Yes X No ___ (w_1=20)	SCALE 2: Suicide Yes ___ No X (w_2=30)	SCALE 3: Manipulation Yes ___ No X (w_3=25)	SCALE 4: Drug Abuse Yes X No ___ (w_4=30)	SCALE 5: Dependency on CIC Yes X No ___ (w_5=10)
a. most unfavorable treatment outcome thought likely (−2)	Patient has made no attempt to enroll in high school.	Patient has committed suicide.	Patient makes rounds of community service agencies demanding medication, and refuses other forms of treatment ✓	Patient reports addiction to "hard narcotics" (heroin, morphine).	Patient has contacted CIC by telephone or in person at least seven times since his first visit.
b. less than expected success with treatment (−1)	Patient has enrolled in high school, but at time of follow-up has dropped out. ✓	Patient has acted on at least one suicidal impulse since her first contact with the CIC, but has not succeeded.	Patient no longer visits CIC with demands for medication but continues with other community agencies and still refuses other forms of treatment.	Patient has used "hard narcotics," but is not addicted, and/or uses hallucinogens (LSD, Pot) more than four times a month. ✓	Patient has contacted CIC 5-6 times since intake.
c. expected level of treatment success (0)	Patient has enrolled, and is in school at follow-up, but is attending class sporadically (misses an average of more than a third of her classes during a week).	Patient reports she has had at least four suicidal impulses since her first contact with the CIC but has not acted on any of them.	Patient no longer attempts to manipulate for drugs at community service agencies, but will not accept another form of treatment. *	Patient has not used "hard narcotics" during follow-up period, and uses hallucinogens between 1-4 times a month. *	Patient has contacted CIC 3-4 times since intake. ✓
d. more than expected success with treatment (+1)	Patient has enrolled, is in school at follow-up, and is attending classes consistently, but has no vocational goals. *		Patient accepts non-medication treatment at some community agency. *	Patient uses hallucinogens less than once a month.	
e. best anticipated success with treatment (+2)	Patient has enrolled, is in school at follow-up, is attending classes consistently, and has some vocational goal.	Patient reports she had no suicidal impulses since her first contact with the CIC.	Patient accepts non-medication treatment, and by own report shows signs of improvement.	At time of follow-up, patient is not using any illegal drugs.	Patient has not contacted CIC since intake. *

is being assessed. Outcome levels were then selected for some scales cases with the patient's involvement, for others only by the clinician. The expected level with treatment on the first scale is tailormade for this patient, indicating some practical steps would be taken by the patient but with some ambivalence. The range of outcomes on either side of this expected outcome are also tailormade, and are within the capability of this patient. The reasoning goes as follows: given this patient, with her background, her environment, her abilities and liabilities and her hopes for the future, and given the capabilities of our treatment staff to treat such cases and the current state of knowledge regarding such cases, what can we expect her to be doing, to be like, at the time of followup?

Since the scales are weighted relative to one another, any set of numbers can be used. The checkmarks indicate the clinician's estimate of the level at intake. The asterisks are the recording of the followup worker. Using the formula derived by Dr. Sherman, a T-score summarizes the outcome for this patient. Comparing the intake with the followup score provides a difference score, or estimate of change during treatment.

The technique appeared to be straightforward but basic questions remained to be answered. NIMH sponsored a program evaluation project in 1969 to determine the characteristics of the measure and to run treatment comparisons in the outpatient unit of the center and to disseminate the method and findings. Some of the questions about the measure to be answered were: (1) was it feasible—will anyone use it, who, in what settings; (2) if it were used, what would be the result—what will be the content of the scales, how reliable is the method, does it make a difference who constructs the followup guide, how does it relate to other measures, what are the characteristics of the score; (3)what good is it—what can the measure be used for, will it make any difference?

The investigative method used by the project was complex but included these features:

1. A followup guide was constructed by an intake worker after one or two interviews with the patient.
2. The patient was randomly assigned to treatment when appropriate.
3. The therapist and patient did not know the contents of the followup guide.
4. The followup guide(s) was scored by a followup worker who was not part of the center staff. He also obtained a consumer satisfaction report.

After three years of the four-year project, some findings relate to the questions listed above. Twenty-five hundred followup guides have been constructed in the outpatient unit, averaging about four scales each. Nine hundred followup interviews have been held. The goal attainment score has a roughly symmetrical distribution, with a mean of 50, a standard deviation of 10, a range of 20 to 80. The correlations between guides constructed independently by different staff at different times is around .70. Agreement between followup workers, independently scoring the same guides, is also approximately .70. A number of reliability studies are in various stages of completion. For instance, scoring reliability is being determined for followup workers of different professions and levels of training, between therapists and followup workers, between phone and in-person followup.

Generally, the advantage of the method lies in its open structure, its ability to accommodate subjective states and unique qualities and to combine these with standard measures. Another presumed advantage is that the method requires that trainees be measured only on dimensions that are believed to be relevant to that trainee. The other presumed advantage is that only the particular range of values within a dimension are chosen, while unlikely extremes are not retained. And finally, particular, objectively determinable outcomes chosen in advance permit audit of the goal setting and perhaps help reduce some of the subjective rater bias involved in global ratings.

The difficulties in using the method relate to its novel aspects. It takes a while to get some people to think in terms of objective outcomes. Also because of the relativistic framework, comparisons across trainee populations and repeated measures over time require additional appraisal of the goals and their outcomes according to the particular value system and standards of the new frame of reference. Technical solutions for this dilemma are planned, and some nearly completed, but every effort to escape the ultimate relativism has so far resulted in only another variety of relativism. Whatever the perspective, including the national viewpoint, the resulting standards always appeared to be just another followup guide, determined for a particular era and society.

The openness of the method may be somewhat baffling. Goal Attainment Scaling is not a scale. Any objective content may be used to judge progress towards any goals. The content need not be the goals themselves but indicators of goal achievement. Those organizations having patients and cultures in common can exchange content lists, develop their own local norms, or develop shared norms. If patient and staff composition is fairly constant, a standard language can be devised (and apparently has been in one setting). The reliabilities will vary with the usage—the content, the rigor with which outcomes are specified, the choice of followup dates, the nature of the followup workers and goal creators.

The costs depend on what you want to do. If you want to check on the accuracy of your own expectations or the outcome of training, it costs practically nothing in terms of equipment, personnel, etc.—about twenty minutes to write a guide and probably another twenty to do a telephone followup (if you don't use a volunteer). If you want to perform training comparisons, the costs depend on the design, method, sample size, type of analysis and questions to be answered.

The score itself has been an issue for some. Some prefer that numbers other than zero stand for expected level, such as a positive integer (with positive implications) or something that fits their intuitive feeling for numbers. Others prefer a number other than 50 to be the central T-score value, such as 70 (for passing) or 100, as in I.Q. scores. Some prefer that the minus two (-2) should be at the bottom of the sheet. Again, it depends on what you want to do. In many cases no numbers at all need be used. Simple inspection might be sufficient. Basically the formula takes into account varying numbers of scales and weights in producing a score that has equal importance for each patient in a sample of patients.

If you are looking for differences in a formal study, the formula will help you find them with a slightly smaller sample. There is some value in selecting procedures that have been used by others, primarily in order to be able to relate your findings to theirs, perhaps taking advantage of norms and measurement characteristics that have already been developed.

Another disadvantage is simply that not enough is known about this style of measure and its applications. In developing about 1,600 contacts, we have received valuable criticism and suggestions; new ideas for application that probably would not have occurred to us. There are about 40 to 50 users and former users, and others in various stages of conducting both formal and informal studies. All of this work is new and exciting, involving considerable ingenuity. All of it, however, has not been around long enough to have received the kind of cautious, thorough, critical peer review that is necessary to understand the work in the context of psychological measurement, and to determine the optimal applications that can be made.

Some questions being investigated are particularly intriguing. Who should and who can set the goals remains to be determined in many settings. Some population groups being tested are disturbed children, delinquent youths, adult prisoners, parolees, adult outpatients, the aged. What are the expectations of professionals for these population groups, of the individuals within these groups for themselves? What are trainees' own expectations? How accurate are these expectations? What effects on outcome do these expectations have? If a trainee devises his own training goals and goal indicators, what effect does this have on the outcome of his treatment?

5

Application of Edwards' Multiattribute Utilities to the Evaluation of Training

MARCIA GUTTENTAG

All decision-theoretic approaches are based on the decisionmaker's subjective answers to two questions: what's at stake and what are the odds (Edwards, 1971). The answer to what's at stake requires the measurement of values and utilities. The answer to what are the odds requires either direct estimation of probabilities or the kind of information processing for which Bayes theorem is the optimal mathematical model.

In Bayesian statistics one compares the subjective hypotheses of the decisionmaker with each other, rather than with the null hypotheses. The probability distributions that are used are the decisionmaker's prior and posterior subjective probabilities.

A difficult question has been how to measure the social utilities of decisionmakers. Some of the technologies proposed for this are cumbersome or unrealistic. The technology for the measurement of multiattribute utilities developed by Edwards (1971) is realistic and can be applied with efficiency.

There are ten steps* that embody this approach to the task of measuring the values of action alternatives. Incidentally, these action alternatives need not be mutually exclusive. Moreover, they need not be prospective actions. If they are actions to be taken in the future, we are talking about the technology of decisionmaking. If they are actions already taken in the past, we are talking about the technology of program-evaluation.

STEP 1

Identify the organization whose utilities are to be maximized. The organization must be identified and its relevant training goals specified. The organization can be represented by appropriate individuals.

STEP 2

Identify the issue or issues to which the utilities needed are relevant. There may be many different, though related, purposes for which utilities are needed. These may include effects of training on trainees, effects of training on those served, etc.

*The ten steps that follow are from an article by W. Edwards that appeared in proceedings of a symposium, Decision and risk analysis—powerful new tools for management. Annapolis, U. S. Naval Academy, June 19, 1971.

To show that these utilities are different, though they may be utilities of the same objects for the same organization, one need only consider dimensions of value relevant to one purpose but not to another.

In general, utility is a triadic relation . . . a function of the evaluator, of the entity being evaluated, and of the purpose for which the evaluation is being made. Most formulations tend to ignore the third argument of the utility function.

STEP 3

Identify the entities (training programs) to be evaluated. In some contexts, the entities to be evaluated are not obvious. "In general, the entities to be evaluated will depend on the nature of the actions being considered. Very often, the entities will be simply those actions themselves. If not, they will relate to those actions in some fairly straightforward way."

STEP 4

Identify the relevant dimensions of value. The first three steps are more or less philosophical. The first answers the question: Whose utility? The second answers the question: Utility for what purpose? The third answers the question: Utility of what entities? With Step 4 we come to the first technical task: discover what dimensions of value are important to the evaluation of the entities we are interested in. Values can be generated by trainees, by the people they serve, by community people, and/or by program directors.

STEP 5

Rank the value dimensions in order of importance. This ranking job is also to be performed by the representatives of the decision-making organization, or by trainees, or by community people. Any or all of these groups may be included in all the steps of the value dimension specifications. Once the list evolved at Step 4 is available, the task is simply to decide which is most important, which next, and so on. Units of measurement are to be ignored at this step. Interpersonal disagreements are very likely at this step.

STEP 6

Rate value dimensions in importance, preserving ratios. To do this start by assigning the least important dimension an importance of 10. (10 rather than 1 is used to permit subsequent judgments to be finely graded and still be made in integers.) Now consider the next least important dimension. How much more important (if at all), is it than the least important? Assign it a number that reflects that ratio. Continue on up the lists, checking each set of implied ratios as each new judgment is made. Thus if a dimension is assigned a weight of 20, while another is assigned a weight of 80, it means that the 20 dimension is ¼ as important as the 80 dimension. And so on. By the time you get to the most important dimensions, there will be many checks to perform; typically, respondents will want to revise previous judgments to make them consistent with present ones. That's fine; they can do so.

Once again, individual differences are likely to arise.

STEP 7

Sum the importance weights, divide each by the sum and multiply by 100. This is a purely computational step which converts importance weights into numbers that, mathematically, are rather like probabilities. The choice of a 0-to-100 scale is, of course, purely arbitrary.

At this step, the folly of including too many dimensions at Step 4 becomes glaringly apparent. If 100 points are to be distributed over a set of dimensions, and some dimensions are very much more important than others, then the less important dimensions will have non-trivial weights only if there aren't too many of them. As a rule of thumb, 8 dimensions is plenty, and 15 is too many. Knowing this, you will want at Step 4 to discourage respondents from being too finely analytical; rather gross dimensions will be just right. Moreover, it may occur that the list of dimensions will be revised later—that revision, if it occurs, will typically consist of including more rather than fewer. Respondents need not worry about the fine shades of difference at Step 4; they can be global in outlook.

STEP 8

Measure the location of each training component or program being evaluated on each dimension. The word 'measure' is used rather loosely here. There are three classes of dimensions: purely subjective, partly subjective and purely objective. The purely subjective dimensions, are perhaps the easiest: you simply get an appropriate expert to estimate the position of each entity on that dimension on a 0-to-100 scale, where 0 is defined as the minimum plausible value on that dimension and 100 is defined as the maximum plausible value. Note "minimum and maximum plausible" rather than "minimum and maximum possible." The minimum plausible value is often not total absence of the dimension. A purely subjective dimension might be the extent to which a training program fulfills the values of trainees.

A partly subjective dimension is one in which the units of measurement are objective, but the locations of the entities must be subjectively estimated. An example might be effects of the training program on trainees, five years after training is completed. Such locations must be subjectively estimated while the program is evaluated.

A wholly objective dimension is one that can be measured rather objectively, in objective units, before the decision. For partly or wholly objective dimensions, it is necessary to have the estimators provide not only values for each entity to be evaluated, but also minimum and maximum plausible values, in the natural units of each dimension.

The final task in Step 8 is to convert measures of the partly subjective and wholly objective dimensions into the 1-to-100 scale in which 0 is minimum plausible and 100 is maximum plausible. A linear transformation is almost always entirely adequate for this purpose.

Now all entities measured are measured and all on the same scale. There is no evidence that the minimum plausible and maximum plausible values somehow define common points on all dimensions—much less that the scale between these points is linear when objective units are involved. They are offered as heuristics that permit one to get on with the job.

STEP 9

Calculate utilities for entities. The equation is

$$U_i = \sum_J w_j u_{ij}$$

remembering that

$$\sum_J w_j = 100$$

U_i is the aggregate utility for the ith entity. w_j is the normalized importance weight of the jth dimension, and u_{ij} is the rescaled position of the ith entity on the jth dimension. Thus w_j emerges from Step 7 and u_{ij} emerges from Step 8.

STEP 10

Decide. If a single act is to be chosen, the rule is simple: maximize U_i. If a subset of i is to be chosen, then the subset for which $\sum_i U_i$ is a maximum is best.

A special case arises when one of the dimensions is cost, and there is a maximum permissible cost—that is, a budget constraint. Under that circumstance, Steps 4 through 10 should be done ignoring the cost dimension. Then the ratios U/C should be calculated, and actions should be chosen in decreasing order of that ratio until the budget constraint is used up. This is the *only* case in which the benefit to cost ratio is an appropriate figure on which to base a decision. More usually, cost is just another dimension of value, to be treated on the same footing as all other dimensions of value. All negative dimensions will, of course, enter into Step 9 with a minus sign, so in effect it is the benefit minus cost difference, not the benefit over cost ratio that should usually control action. Indeed this whole approach can easily be adapted to cases in which there are minimum or maximum acceptable values on a given dimension of value, by simply excluding action alternatives that transgress these limits.

The power of the multiattribute utility lies in its thoroughgoing subjectivity. It begins by having the various participants in the training process state their values, and then all training programs or subentities in training programs are evaluated according to these explicitly stated values.

This approach can also be used in the planning of training programs. Only those programs can be chosen which, on an *a priori* basis, maximize the value of the participants. After training programs have been instituted, the aspects of the training program which are to be evaluated are determined by these dimensions for which one requires objective measurement.

The evaluation research plan is the outcome of the values-recommendations matrix. Those recommendations—in this case, those aspects of the training programs which are judged to be high on the subjective scale of maximum plausible value—are the ones which are investigated. Thus the values which underlie the program determine which aspects of the program should be investigated. Using the multiattribute utility approach, it is possible to substitute objective measures for the initially subjective measures on the minimum-to-maximum plausible scale of value, and therefore to show the extent to which the values of the program were actually realized.

One other aspect of the use of multiattribute utilities should be noted. This method permits groups which have different values in respect to the training program to preserve the integrity of each different value position. In that case, steps 4 through 9 are conducted independently for each of these groups. Each group independently judges programs on their own subjective scales of maximum-to-minimum plausible value. Later, when objective evaluation information is available to feed back to each group, the same information is used independently to revise each group's subjective scaling. Value differences are preserved. Using the same objective evaluation data from a single training program, groups which began with different value systems, can reach very different conclusions about the program's worth.

Part III

Conclusions

6

Review of the History of the Evaluation of Training in Psychology

Background

During the 1950s clinical and counseling psychologists became convinced that mental health involved more than the absence of mental illness, and that preoccupation with the mentally ill was preventing psychologists from giving the needed attention to the full range of community mental health problems. The Mental Health Study Act of 1955 set up a commission which was directed to make recommendations for a national health program. The final report of the commission noted that manpower resources were severely limited, that mental health services for children and racial and ethnic minorities were lacking and that services were not available at times of major crises and only minimally available to the poor. It therefore recommended that new mental health facilities be established in community settings, that educational and consultative services be greatly expanded and that research and preventative efforts be intensified. These recommendations were embodied in legislation proposed by John F. Kennedy and were passed as part of the Mental Health Facilities Act of 1963. The act provided funds for the construction of comprehensive community mental health centers throughout the nation; in essence the arena for treatment was now moved from the mental hospital to the community.

Yet the shift in actual emphasis of the community mental health center did not occur until the mid-1960s. At the Boston Conference (Bennet, 1966) a broader conception of education of psychologists in community mental health evolved. Believing that it was no longer sufficient to deal with the mental health problems of individuals who were the casualties of the system, it facilitated a shift from community mental health to community psychology by emphasizing prevention of mental illness. A year after the Boston Conference, the American Psychological Association issued its first position paper. Pointing to the need for representatives of the community to be actively involved in a program which should promote positive mental health as well as prevent and treat mental illness, it focused its attention on psychologists. It noted that with few exceptions, the graduate training of psychologists has contained little that would help them work effectively in the community. Consequently, if psychologists are to be involved in community affairs, graduate education in psychology must provide students with opportunities to learn about communities as social systems and to understand the socio-political realities that confront those who work in community settings.

As clinical programs opened to the mental health fields, courses and programs in community psychology were offered to enable the students to obtain the necessary skills for the new roles that had to be assumed. These roles include mental health consultants, participant-conceptualizers, and social change agents (Iscoe & Spielberger, 1970) and mental health quarterback and social engineer (Cowen, 1970b). In view of the many new professional roles for psychologists in community settings, Division 27 of the APA established a task force to clarify community mental health goals and priorities. A report submitted in 1969 specifically recommended that university psychology departments give the highest priority to training psychologists who are competent to design, execute, and be accountable for collaborative social interventions.

With the shift in emphasis to train professionals to work in the community, it became apparent that there would be a shortage of highly trained mental personnel and a low likelihood that the training centers could expand sufficiently to meet the foreseeable needs. Thus, it became necessary to develop new sources of manpower. However, while psychologists may have turned to nonprofessionals "more out of desperation than out of conceptualization," that is not to say that the nonprofessional may actually offer unique and much needed services that the professional may be less apt to supply (Cowen, 1969, p. 371). Indeed, nonprofessionals may be closer in lifestyle to the people with whom they work and therefore may be able to empathize and communicate better with the clients than some professionals. Further, they may bring an enthusiasm and optimism to their jobs that a seasoned professional may, to some extent, have lost.

In setting up programs to provide professionals and nonprofessionals with skills and tools necessary to deal with the casualties of the social system, and to begin to unravel the complexities of the social system that produces these casualties, it became vital to evaluate all training efforts. The evaluation component of a program would mark progress toward specific goals of the community mental health program and would also provide new information. A training program could be evaluated by direct and indirect measures. For example, if a mental health center evaluates the rate of improvement of mental health in the community, it is indirectly evaluating its efforts in training, since presumably the improved training of the staff may have contributed to the improved health of the community. However, such an indirect measure is not the same as a measure which would evaluate the specific training procedures by noting the direct change in the trainee as a result of the training.

At this point it must be stated that psychology was not alone in being concerned about the emphasis of their services. Numerous other professions, such as psychiatry, social work and nursing, equally recognized the need to become community-oriented. However, to date very little information concerning the efforts of these professions to train professionals and nonprofessionals for community mental health has been located. Therefore, it becomes virtually impossible to write anything substantial about their efforts. For this reason, the material that follows will be concerned with the efforts and lack of efforts psychologists have made to evaluate training for community mental health. Thus, the information presented may or may not serve as a model for what is also going on in professions other than psychology. Once more information is made available concerning the efforts of these other professions to evaluate training; it will be included and will restore the balance to the picture that unfortunately cannot be presented here.

RECOGNITION, BUT NOT ACTION

While the shift from clinical treatment to community psychology began almost two decades ago, the importance of evaluation in training programs has yet to be fully recognized. When Bloom reported to the Institute on Psychological Training (1969), he could report that there was an increased participation of psychologists in community action programs. However, he also noted that a "lack of conceptual clarity and methodological rigor characterized these efforts." In his own words, "the spirit of inquiry seems to have been displaced by the call to action, and it is highly problematical whether a field of activity characterized by action without evaluation can become a permanent member of the academic community" (p. 8). Recognition of the importance of evaluation, and yet of its absence from community mental health programs, was also reported by Smith and Hobbs (1966) in an American Psychological Association position paper. They wrote:

> The comprehensive community mental health center should devote an explicit portion of its budget to program evaluation. All centers should inculcate in their staff attention to and respect for research findings; the larger centers have an obligation to set a high priority for basic research and give formal recognition to research as a legitimate part of the duties of staff members. . . . In the 11 "model" community programs which have been cited previously, both program evaluation and basic research are rarities; staff members have been overburdened by their service obligations. . . . The programs of social agencies are seldom evaluated systematically and tend to continue in operation simply because they exist and no one has data to demonstrate whether they are useful or not. . . . Only through explicit appraisal of program effects can worthy approaches be retained and refined, ineffective ones dropped [pp. 21–22].

In reference to graduate education in community psychology, just one of the arenas of training mental health workers, Spielberger and Iscoe (1971) remark on the necessity to evaluate current and future programs:

> Since community psychology lacks at present a coherent body of knowledge of its own and an

established set of practices, there are as yet few meaningful precedents upon which to base graduate training programs in the field. To establish a viable community psychology that will meet the growing needs for an ever broader spectrum of psychological research and services in community settings, radical modification of existing graduate programs in psychology will be required, or entirely new training programs must be created.

Finally, an analysis of projects that have been, or are now, underway in training personnel for various community mental health positions, as discussed in *Community Psychology: Perspectives in Training and Research* (Iscoe and Spielberger, 1970) and *Project Summaries of Experiments in Mental Health Training* (National Institute for Mental Health, 1971) will demonstrate how little actual attention has been paid to evaluation in many training programs that have existed and do exist.

Nevertheless, there are projects that have employed various techniques and tools to evaluate aspects of their training programs. If future programs are to employ a sophisticated evaluation component, then it is of paramount importance that we know the present procedures for evaluating community mental health training and the aspects of training being evaluated.

Evaluation Efforts

Levy et al. state that "one of the first requirements of evaluation research in a state agency is the need to develop a conceptual model of the evaluative process so as to avoid being overwhelmed by the enormous variety of data that affect our activities" (1968, p. 341). The same is true for the community health center or the university which provides the education for the mental health worker. First the center must define its own system by stating its goals and objectives. Then it can establish the criteria by which to evaluate the training program.

The Department of Health, Education and Welfare set up the following general criteria for a training program:

1. Program significance or relevance:
   a. Does the program meet a special need?
   b. Does the program meet educational development needs (i.e., in relation to the long-term view needs of the field)?
2. Program category (included here are the clinical doctoral psychology training programs in universities, field training center programs, and applied programs other than clinical).
3. Innovative features in the program.
4. Minority group recruitment and training efforts.
5. Regional need.
6. Breadth of training.
7. Exposure to other disciplines in the training to professionals and nonprofessionals.
8. Program productivity.

The NIMH *Guidelines for Evaluation of Continuing Education Programs in Mental Health* stresses the evaluation of vested interests. It includes in this category the following: (1) the community, (2) the trainees, (3) the sponsoring organization, (4) the program director and staff and (5) the funding organization. Evaluation researchers have established other sets of criteria. James (1962), for example, believes that the following criteria should be used: measures of effort, performance, adequacy of performance and efficiency.

TYPES OF EVALUATION

Three of the most common types of evaluation are outcome, process and structure. Outcome measures determine whether or not the trainee and the services he renders have altered. Process evaluation is concerned with measuring how appropriately and how well the methods of training are applied. Structure evaluation examines the tools necessary to provide the training. For more details on these types of evaluation see Donabedian, 1966, and Zusman et al., 1969.

Unfortunately, most training programs have not been engaged in evaluating their programs. Therefore it is of interest to see what types of evaluations and what criteria procedures and tools are, in fact, used. Since it has been found that the information available can be described in general terms, examples of some evaluation programs will be provided to give concrete illustrations.

University Settings

In the two- and four-year college programs there

appear to be three basic goals that most programs share: (1) to provide a broad educational background, (2) to provide sufficient education in the specific mental health skills and tools that the student will need to become a mental health worker and (3) to provide practicum experience for the worker-to-be. To accomplish these goals, specific objectives are set by the university or college administrators. Some of the more common ones are: to provide a wide range of course materials pertaining to the mental health field; to provide the best possible faculty; to provide top-quality courses; to provide the broadest possible base for working in the community (such as by providing an interdisciplinary staff and set of courses for the program); to provide a variety of practicum experiences with the agencies and the community mental health centers; to provide the best possible funding opportunities for students; and to provide places of employment for the graduates.

METHODS

Evaluations concerning the structure of the program, its processes and outcome, when done at all, are generally descriptive. The Southern Regional Education Board, for example, reports in its status report of 1971, that of the community colleges surveyed, very few have done any evaluation work (though more are now planning to do so), but that the evaluations made generally consist of asking for recommendations from the graduates about the structure of the program and for feedback concerning what aspects of their training had been most useful to them. In a number of universities and colleges, the students and the graduates are asked to evaluate the curriculum, the staff, the practicum experiences and their attitudes toward various aspects of the program, either in interviews, in group sessions or by completing questionnaires. Often staff and administrators are informally asked for their comments. Probably the most popular evaluation is that of "determining the ease or difficulty with which our graduates secure employment opportunities" in the mental health community. Thus, Stewart (1972) reports that his university sends questionnaires to graduates to evaluate the training program as well as their current employment status.

Hill (1971) reports the following method was used to evaluate graduate training in sociology. Interviews were conducted with all faculty members having significant responsibility for graduate-level training, and specifically research training. Questionnaires were sent out to all students who had graduated from the program. The questionnaire consisted of two checklists. In the first were thirty-one experience items, in the second were forty-eight methodological topics (see tables 6.1 and 6.2). The students were asked to report their exposure to or experience with the topics and procedures. The faculty in turn was asked to judge the importance of the various items with respect to training. (Hill reports that there was a striking correspondence between faculties' ratings of importance and the probability that the student was exposed to the subject matter.)

CONTENT

A program which is presently underway, but has not yet published its data, provides an example of the

Table 6.1
FACULTY JUDGMENTS OF EXPERIENCE AND GRADUATE STUDENTS
REPORTS OF EXPERIENCE FOR 31 RESEARCH EXPERIENCES

Research Experience	Percent of Faculty Saying All Graduate Students Should Have Experience At Least Once (N=222)	Percent of Graduate Students Reporting Having Had Experience At Least Once (N=1171)[1]
1. Writing a research report	97.3	66.1[2]
2. Preparing a research proposal	83.8	83.5
3. Designing a questionnaire	80.7	91.1
4. Coding questionnaire or interview material	74.3	89.1
5. Administering a questionnaire	73.0	89.8
6. Constructing a simple causal model	72.9	68.7
7. Interviewing in the field	68.0	81.6
8. Using a computer in analyzing data	68.0	76.5
9. Submitting a paper for publication	57.2	27.2[3]
10. Presenting a paper at a professional meeting	56.3	20.4
11. Replicating a piece of research	45.5	35.2
12. Interviewing in an office or interviewing room	45.0	53.5
13. Making observations in the field as an "identified" observer	41.9	49.5
14. Designing a sampling plan for a large scale survey	41.4	45.3
15. Analyzing institutional or organizational records	31.5	42.5
16. Making observations in the field as a "concealed" observer	31.1	39.6

Table 6.1 continued
FACULTY JUDGMENTS OF EXPERIENCE AND GRADUATE STUDENTS
REPORTS OF EXPERIENCE FOR 31 RESEARCH EXPERIENCES

Research Experience	Percent of Faculty Saying All Graduate Students Should Have Experience At Least Once (N=222)	Percent of Graduate Students Reporting Having Had Experience At Least Once (N=1171)[1]
17. Submitting a grant application for research funds	30.7	31.1
18. Working with field informants	28.4	41.8
19. Making a case study	27.9	43.4
20. Performing a content analysis	27.0	45.5
21. Writing a computer program	26.6	46.1
22. Using data archives or banks	26.6	25.3
23. Training interviewers	25.7	28.3
24. Conducting an experiment in a small-group laboratory	24.8	21.4
25. Analyzing historical documents	21.7	34.5
26. Training observers	19.0	11.4
27. Doing a cohort analysis	18.0	18.1
28. Supervising a survey research team	14.5	21.2
29. Living in a field setting while collecting data	12.2	21.6
30. Becoming a member of a "natural" group for research purposes	11.3	14.3
31. Acting as an accomplice or "stooge" in a laboratory experiment	7.2	15.6

[1]Omits responses from 38 students who had not completed one full year of graduate school.

[2]Research reports written as class assignments were excluded.

[3]18.4 percent of these 1,171 respondents have had at least one paper published.

[4]r_{12}=.8413. If items 1, 7 and 10 are omitted, r_{12}=.9496.

Table 6.2
FACULTY JUDGMENTS REGARDING COVERAGE THAT SHOULD BE
GIVEN TO 48 METHODOLOGICAL TOPICS, AND GRADUATE STUDENT EXPERIENCE
WITH THESE TOPICS

Methodological Topic [1]	Percent of Faculty Saying Topic Should Receive Some Discussion In Courses Taken By All Graduate Students (N=222)	Percent of Graduate Students Reporting At Least Some Exposure to Topic (N=1,171) [2]
1. Experimental design	95.9	94.2
2. Analysis of variance	93.7	94.6
3. Nonparametric statistical tests	93.7	89.7
4. Multiple regression analysis	89.6	83.9
5. Stratified sampling	88.3	93.1
6. Construction of codes for interviews or questionnaires	86.4	90.6
7. Cluster sampling	85.6	83.8
8. Structured interviewing methods	84.7	93.9
9. Analysis of covariance	84.7	85.6
10. Computer methods for data analysis	78.8	75.7
11. Likert scale construction	76.6	84.4
12. Factor analysis	76.2	83.1
13. Panel designs	76.2	70.0
14. Item analysis	73.9	65.0
15. Sequential sampling	73.9	53.5
16. Path analysis	73.4	62.0
17. Scalogram analysis	71.6	68.7
18. Content analysis	70.8	80.5
19. Use of dummy variables	70.3	57.4
20. Nonparticipant observation techniques	68.5	83.8
21. Participant observation techniques	67.4	90.6
22. Analytic induction	64.9	50.5
23. Depth-interviewing methods	64.4	81.1
24. Paired-comparison scale construction	63.5	59.6
25. Crosscultural comparative methods	61.7	79.8
26. Equal-appearing interval scale construction	61.7	68.7

Table 6.2 continued

FACULTY JUDGMENTS REGARDING COVERAGE THAT SHOULD BE
GIVEN TO 48 METHODOLOGICAL TOPICS, AND GRADUATE STUDENT EXPERIENCE
WITH THESE TOPICS

Methodological Topic[1]	Percent of Faculty Saying Topic Should Receive Some Discussion In Courses Taken By All Graduate Students (N=222)	Percent of Graduate Students Reporting At Least Some Exposure to Topic (N=1,171)[2]
27. Multidimensional scaling methods	58.1	46.5
28. Computer methods for data storage and retrieval	53.6	52.8
29. Cluster analysis	52.2	35.8
30. Semantic differential	51.8	57.5
31. Computer user languages	49.1	67.7
32. Discriminant function analysis	46.8	15.5
33. Collection of life-history materials	45.5	66.2
34. Analysis of sociometric choice data	44.6	69.0
35. Ethnomethodology	43.3	57.6
36. Maximum likelihood estimation techniques	42.4	26.6
37. Coding small-group interaction	41.0	71.9
38. Analysis of historical documents	36.5	62.4
39. Analysis of personal documents	34.2	58.7
40. Computer simulation strategies	30.6	32.4
41. Markov processes	30.6	33.0
42. Smallest space analysis	29.3	12.8
43. Graph theoretical methods	27.5	23.3
44. Monte Carlo techniques	27.5	19.6
45. Canonical correlation	26.1	17.0
46. Construction of life tables	24.3	40.2
47. Linguistic analysis	18.1	31.4
48. Computer assembly languages	17.6	15.0

[1]$r_{12}=.8329$
[2]Omits responses from 38 students who had not completed 1 full year of graduate school.

type of evaluation work that could be done. Hadley et al. (1970) reports on a program at Purdue that is planning several aspects of research:

> The first is designated as process research. This phase attempts to answer the question of whether the attitudes and behavior which are to be hypothesized to be health engendering are, in fact, being developed. Outcome research concerned with the evaluation of the students' performance in work settings and of the impact and functioning of the graduates is contemplated. Base-line data is being accumulated concerning the activities being conducted by existing personnel on mental health settings. Similar data will be accumulated when the graduates enter these or similar settings. The entire question of what are health engendering attitudes and behaviors is being studied. Assuming that change does occur in the students, it is necessary to determine what variables are responsible for the change. [p. 50]

Many of the four-year university training programs, when asked to report on their evaluation data, produced a summary of courses involved in the program, as if to say "we should evaluate ourselves only by the quantity (and presumably quality) of courses we offer our students." Kelley, for one, finds even this one criterion (which would be considered insufficient as the only evaluation measure) unacceptable: "To my mind, the criteria for training would be shifted from defining units of courses to creating segments of training. In sum, the student would participate in training until that particular activity is completed—when the particular segment is achieved" (1970, p. 527).

Cowen, who has been involved with a number of preventive mental health programs sponsored by the University of Rochester, all of which have used questionnaires and interviews to evaluate the process or outcome of the program, has noted a possible weakness in the clinical psychology doctoral programs. Noting that the practicum experiences for this program usually take place in the fourth year, he observes that this has two advantages: (1) students by this time have acquired considerable clinical background and experience in a variety of settings and (2) if practicum experiences are taken soon after completion of Ph.D. degree, the likelihood that they will carry over to one's post-Ph.D. activities is increased. However, he notes these advantages may be outweighed by the disadvantages: (1) the experience occurs so late in the student's training that there is little room for building on it, (2) program followthrough is hampered because the student will shortly leave the area and (3) there is heavy competing pressure from other vital activities (e.g., the Ph.D. dissertation) that rules out anything approaching full immersion in the community mental health practicum assignment.

Community Mental Health Centers

Programs in the community mental health centers are designed to train nonprofessionals, or to provide continuing education for the professionals. Therefore, the length of the training period can range from a matter of weeks to years. The general goals of these

programs are the same as those of the university settings except that much less emphasis is placed on providing a broad educational background since the professional already has it, and the time is too short to
concentrate on this aspect with the nonprofessional.
The specific objectives usually are: to give the mental
health worker the necessary skills to work with the
clients, the professionals and the community agencies;
to provide these skills in the most efficient way possible; and to provide continuing education for those
mental health workers for whom it is necessary.

METHODS

Whereas most of the evaluative methods used in
the university settings rely on interviews and some-
times questionnaires, community mental health centers rarely use interviews as the main questionnaires;
log book entries, visual and audio tapes and even standardized measures are used. Whereas evaluation in
the universities and colleges is mostly concerned with
structure and outcome, in the community mental
health centers there is also concern with process evaluation.

Levine (1972) reported the following method for
evaluating an in-hospital community college program.
Attendants who had left their hospital positions to
serve as students in a training course were asked to sit
in on precourse evaluation meetings. At these meetings they made suggestions concerning the evaluation
of the program that they were now to begin. As a result
of these meetings, a questionnaire was designed and
then administered to the supervisors of these attendants to determine their attitudes toward the pro-

gram. Once the training program was completed, questionnaires were administered to the supervisors (again), the teachers and the patients to determine their attitudes toward various aspects of the now-completed program. Students made self-reports of motivation and commitment to the program and gave indications as to how their lives and self-images were changed by the program. In addition, the evaluation design had a control group: a group of attendants who did not take the training program.

Geis (1968) described the evaluation techniques used to monitor a training course offered juvenile court judges, and assessed their utility. While the specific program does not fall within the jurisdiction of the report, the techniques used are similar to ones used in some community mental health centers. In this program, log books were maintained by participants, evaluation inquiries were submitted beforehand by the teachers, and pre- and post-questionnaires requesting biographical data, expectations from the program, patterns of work and opinions concerning diverse aspects of the job were completed by the students.

CONTENT

Kriegman et al. (1968) provide an excellent example of the content of a continuing education program. The program was designed to develop a multidisciplinary education program for allied mental health personnel. The program consisted of three projects. In the first, 12 two-hour sessions were held weekly to discuss general mental health problems. After each one-hour lecture by a psychiatrist, participants broke up into small discussion groups. At the conclusion of the course the participants were given a 60-question multiple-choice final examination. Also, leaders of discussion groups were asked to complete questionnaires to provide feedback on the structure of the lectures and the process of the discussion groups. In the second, a three-day workshop, the evaluation procedure consisted of giving participants a 30-question multiple-choice test before and after the course. Instructors were also asked to evaluate the project. In the third project, an eight-week session consisted of lectures, closed television presentations and small discussion groups at each meeting. The discussion groups were matched for a number of variables (such as distribution of educational levels) and were then evaluated according to leader behavior, group interaction and individual behavior. Audio tapes were evaluated in terms of depth of cognitive and affective learning, analysis of group processes, comparison of scoring-sheet data and interaction analysis. A 30-question multiple-choice test was used to evaluate prior knowledge and the learning process.

Finney (in NIMH, 1971) reports that the Woodlawn Organization, which is training indigenous community leaders to provide direct services and serve as catalysts for increased community participation and concern, has no evaluation data available. However, he reported:

> Evaluation will focus on improved mental health of the community emanating from the activities of the personnel trained under this project; the improved mental health of the community will

be assessed by means of a number of indices of social disorganization on a "before and after" basis with the comparative data from other communities in which the program is not available. [p. 18]

Discussion

A review of the literature and the reports from community mental health centers contacted for this report indicates that, in general, there have been very few evaluations of training programs. Those programs that have taken place vary greatly in quality: some have used one or two single measures, others have used multiple measures; some have used descriptive data alone, some have combined descriptive and analytic data. Many of the programs that have evaluation components, have not gone into a great deal of detail as to their content and procedures, making it difficult for other community mental health centers to profit from the experiences of the others. However, the review of the literature and reports does show that there are numerous issues which need to be discussed and analyzed if, in fact, better evaluation procedures are to emerge.

COMPLETENESS

Baker (1969) observed that "the organization that best fits the task of training residents is not necessarily the same one that best fits the task of returning patients to the community" (p. 405). In many of the cases where evaluation is conducted, only a few of the potential aspects of the training program are ever actually evaluated. For example, using a criterion of "the ease or difficulty with which our graduates secure relevant employment opportunities" does not tell whether the graduate will work effectively in the community mental health center with administrators, clients or professionals or nonprofessionals, depending upon which he is. The problems of nonprofessionals with clients and professionals have led to the publication of numerous articles concerning suggestions to improve the training program (e.g., Reisman, 1967). Kaplan et al. (1968) provide an example of a case where professionals had difficulties relating to the clients. In fact, many of the programs described above, which are among the more advanced when it comes to applying evaluation strategies, also commit this error of only evaluating some of the components and not all of them. An evaluation program must be concerned with the structure, the process and the outcome of the program, and must consider the various aspects of the training program that are relevant before, during and after the actual training has taken place.

MONETARY ISSUES

Smith and Hobbs (1966) made the following observation:

> One approach to program evaluation is hard-headed cost analysis. Alternative programs should be compared not only in terms of their effects but what they cost. Since almost any approach to service is likely to produce some good effects, mental health professionals may be prone to use methods they find most satisfying

rather than those that yield the greatest return to the dollar. [p. 23]

Two issues are brought out here. The first is the issue of cost. Cost per client or cost per trainee are issues rarely mentioned in those evaluations that have been conducted. Yet there is no denying that money for such programs is not always simple to obtain. Second is the issue of cost effectiveness. Zusman and Ross (1969) say that cost effectiveness asks the question, "If program A costs more but is also more effective than program B, which should be used?" These are issues which need to be considered, but probably have not been, due to two factors: (1) the still relative scarcity of evaluations of programs and their anonymity to most professionals and (2) the lack of any standardized measures which can be used by a variety of programs.

One may also ask, what is the proper proportion of a budget that should be spent on evaluation? Smith and Hobbs (1966) answer that question by stating, "as a rough yardstick every center should devote between 5 and 10% of its budget to program evaluation and research." Goldfarb (1967) is one of the very few who mentions the percentage of the budget spent on evaluation and research; he reports that the San Mateo County Mental Health Center spends 10 percent of its budget on evaluation and research.

Another center that has had some interest in financial matters is the Cheyenne Mental Health Center. Hinkle et al. (1969) report that they have an evaluation team which consists of four consultants who are directly responsible to the executive director. One consultant serves as coordinator, one specializes in research design, the third specializes in role and educational problems, and the fourth serves as data collector and computer specialist. The total cost is less than $10,000, and Hinkle reports that "if they hired a full time research specialist and get him assistance, it would mean more expense probably and less variety of backgrounds and skills." In other words, this mental health center has shown its concern for cost efficiency and has described its evaluative researchers better than most other programs in the literature.

INSTRUMENTS

In almost all cases, the evaluators have relied on self-made scales and questionnaires to determine the effectiveness of the particular training program, or the trainee's attitudes toward aspects of it. However, the need for some sort of standardized tools has not been discussed. Some evaluation efforts have produced questionnaires or scales, some of which can, in modified form, be of potential use to other community mental health centers.

Baker and Schulberg (1967) developed a scale which enables evaluators to see the ideological stance taken by the trainees on a "humanism versus custodialism" scale. The scale consists of the following item categories: (1) a population focus, (2) primary intervention, (3) social treatment goals, (4) comprehensive continuity of care and (5) total community involvement (see table 6.3). For example, an administration of such a scale to mental health workers before their training begins, after their practicum experience, after they graduate and after a few years of working, could provide data concerning the effects of these variables on the person's attitudes toward mental health.

Table 6.3
COMMUNITY MENTAL HEALTH IDEOLOGY (CMHI) SCALE

Item	Mean	S.D.	F-loading	Item-total r
1. Every mental health center should have formally associated with it a local citizen's board assigned significant responsibilities.	5.58	1.46	.59	.57
*2. Our time-tested pattern of diagnosing and treating individual patients is still the optimal way for us to function professionally.	4.91	1.95	.61	.61
*3. With our limited professional resources it makes more sense to use established knowledge to treat the mentally ill rather than trying to deal with the social conditions which may cause mental illness.	4.97	1.78	.68	.67
4. Our responsibility for patients extends beyond the contact we have with them in the mental health center.	6.01	1.27	.56	.54
5. A significant part of the psychiatrist's job consists of finding out who the mentally disordered are and where they are located in the community.	4.08	2.04	.44	.44
*6. Such public health programs as primary preventive services are still of little value to the mental health field.	5.04	1.80	.51	.48
7. A mental health program should direct particular attention to groups of people who are potentially vulnerable to upsetting pressures.	5.70	1.51	.45	.44
*8. The planning and operation of mental health programs are professional functions which should not be influenced by citizen pressures.	4.93	1.98	.49	.49
9. Mental health programs should give a high priority to lowering the rate of new cases in a community by reducing harmful environmental conditions.	5.46	1.66	.48	.47
10. The mental health specialist should seek to extend his effectiveness by working through other people.	6.48	.92	.55	.53
*11. A mental health professional can only be responsible for the mentally ill who come to him; he cannot be responsible for those who do not seek him out.	4.71	2.01	.66	.65
12. Out program emphasis should be shifted from the clinical model, directed at specific patients, to the public health model, focusing upon populations.	4.43	1.93	.61	.60
13. Understanding of the community in which we work should be made a central focus in the training of mental health professionals.	6.16	1.21	.57	.55
*14. The control of mental illness is a goal that can only be attained through psychiatric treatment.	5.75	1.58	.53	.51
15. A mental health professional assumes responsibility not only for his current caseload but also for unidentified potentially maladjusted people in the community.	5.16	1.86	.50	.47
16. Our current emphasis upon the problems of individual patients is a relatively ineffective approach for easing a community's total psychiatric problem.	5.03	1.94	.51	.51
*17. Our professional mandate is to treat individual patients and not the harmful influences in society.	5.31	1.81	.67	.65
*18. Our efforts to involve citizens in mental health programs have not produced sufficient payoff to make it worth our while.	5.58	1.52	.56	.54
19. The locus of mental illness must be viewed as extending beyond the individual, and into the family, the community, and the society.	6.38	1.16	.51	.50
*20. Mental health professionals can be concerned for their patients' welfare only when having them in active treatment.	5.92	1.48	.57	.55
21. Mental health consultation is a necessary service which we must provide to community caregivers who can help in the care of the mentally ill.	6.40	.97	.51	.48

(continued on next page)

Table 6.3 (continued)
COMMUNITY MENTAL HEALTH IDEOLOGY (CMHI) SCALE

Item	Mean	S.D.	F-loading	Item-total r
22. Caregiving agents who worked with the patient before and during his contact at the mental health centers should be included in the formulation of treatment plans.	6.34	.95	.51	.48
*23. A psychiatrist can only provide useful services to those people with whom he has direct personal contact.	5.85	1.60	.53	.51
*24. Skill in collaborating with nonmental health professionals is relatively unimportant to the success of our work with the mentally ill.	6.17	1.26	.57	.55
25. The mental health center is only one part of a comprehensive community mental health program.	6.43	.83	.53	.51
*26. Mental health professionals should only provide their services to individuals whom society defines as mentally ill or who voluntarily seek these services.	5.30	1.90	.68	.67
27. We should deal with people who are not yet sick by helping them to develop ways for coping with expected life difficulties.	5.85	1.47	.59	.56
*28. We should not legitimately be concerned with modifying aspects of our patient's environment but rather in bolstering his ability to cope with it.	5.08	1.95	.48	.48
*29. It is a poor treatment policy to allow non-psychiatrists to perform traditional psychiatric functions.	4.88	2.02	.55	.55
*30. Since we do not know enough about prevention, mental health programs should direct their prime efforts toward treating the mentally ill rather than developing prevention programs.	5.47	1.71	.64	.62
31. The hospital and community should strive for the goal of each participating in the affairs and activities of the other.	6.11	1.21	.53	.51
32. Social action is required to insure the success of mental health programs.	6.30	1.11	.47	.44
*33. In view of the professional manpower shortage, existing resources should be used for treatment programs rather than prevention programs.	5.42	1.76	.51	.49
34. Each mental health center should join the health and welfare council of each community it serves.	6.33	1.01	.51	.48
35. The responsible mental health professional should become an agent for social change.	5.27	1.71	.68	.66
*36. We can make more effective use of our skills by intensively treating a limited number of patients instead of working indirectly with many patients.	5.06	1.84	.58	.58
*37. By and large, the practice of good psychiatry does not require very much knowledge about sociology and anthropology.	5.74	1.64	.44	.44
*38. Community agencies working with the patient should not be involved with the different phases of a patient's hospitalization.	5.90	1.36	.56	.53

*Negatively oriented disagree items.

Moos and Otto(1972) have designed a scale that would provide an opportunity to assess the goals or value orientations of members and staff with respect to their conceptualizations of an ideal treatment program (see table 6.4).

Kiresuk and Sherman have designed a Goal Attainment Scale to provide an indicator of therapeutic outcome that would be flexible, practical and useful for evaluative purposes. Since the scale requires that the mental health worker make a followup guide for the client, it is possible to use the worker's scales over a period of time to show any changes that may have taken place in the worker's conception of goals for the clients.

EXPERIMENTATION

Training practices vary from university to university, from community college to community college and from mental health center to mental health center. Comparisons of different contents and methods of training must be made to find the advantages and disadvantages of specific systems. For example, Rioch (1963) has suggested that two years of halftime training may be better than one year of fulltime training. It remains to be tested whether or not this suggestion, like many other such suggestions, is indeed correct. However, there seems to be no effort to take the numerous suggestions that are scattered through the literature and determine adequacies of performance and efficiencies of programs. Larson et al. (1969) have taken a step toward advocating comparing the various training practices which exist:

Table 6.4

COMMUNITY-ORIENTED PROGRAMS ENVIRONMENT SCALES
(COPES): DESCRIPTIONS OF SUBSCALES

1. Program involvement	Measures how active members are in the day-to-day functioning of their program Members put a lot of energy into what they do around here Members here really try to improve and get better
2. Support	Measures the extent to which members are encouraged and supported by staff and other members The healthier members here help take care of the less healthy ones Staff go out of their way to help members
3. Spontaneity	Measures the extent to which the program encourages members to act openly and express their feelings openly Members say anything they want to the staff Members are encouraged to show their feelings
4. Autonomy	Assesses how self-sufficient and independent members are encouraged to be in making their own decisions The staff act on members' suggestions Members are expected to take leadership here
5. Practical orientation	Assesses the extent to which the member's environment orients him toward preparing himself for release from the program This program emphasizes training for new kinds of jobs Members are encouraged to plan for the future
6. Personal problem orientation	Measures the extent to which members are encouraged to be concerned with their personal problems and feelings and to seek to understand them Members tell each other about their personal problems Staff are mainly interested in learning about members' feelings
7. Anger and aggression	Measures the extent to which a member is allowed and encouraged to argue with members and staff, to become openly angry, and to display other aggressive behavior Members often gripe Staff here think it is a healthy thing to argue
8. Order and organization	Measures how important activity planning and neatness is in the program Members' activities are carefully planned The staff make sure that this place is always neat
9. Program clarity	Measures the clarity of goal expectations and rules If a member breaks a rule, he knows what will happen to him
10. Staff control	Assesses the extent to which the staff determines rules Once a schedule is arranged for a member, the member must follow it Everyone knows who's in charge here

*From Moos, R. & Otto, Jean. Community oriented programs. Environment scale: a methodology for facilitation. Evaluation of social change. *C.M.H.J.*, 1972, *8*, (1), 28–37.

Evaluation procedures which test the effectiveness of preventive programs can be developed and conducted more easily in the more structured community of a college or a university than in the less structured community catchment areas. Thus, the college community can provide a proving ground for these programs. Compared to the community catchment area, a college population is smaller, more homogeneous, and relatively stable, with demographic data readily available. Information reflecting student distress can be obtained from academic, counseling, health, and disciplinary records. [p. 463]

The above is a summary of past practices and viewpoints on the evaluation of mental health training.

7

Issues and Recommendations

1. In the evaluation of training in community mental health centers, the effects of training on client care and on the population served is critical, not just the effects of training on trainees. It is the effects on the target which are the most important of the goals of training, and although both trainee and effects of trainee on client are to be studied, the client care is the most important goal.

2. It is essential to determine the values of all participants in the training program. The values and goals of all participants at every level should be specified. The definition of the objectives and values of participants and decisionmakers in the training process, is critical.

3. A network analysis should be done before any evaluation. This network analysis would include all of the systems which have a direct or indirect impingement on the training program itself. Thus, it would include state, county, hospital, department, university and patient level. Housing, the social welfare system and education are also closely linked with the effect of training in community mental health.

4. The outcomes of evaluation should influence future goal-setting.

RECOMMENDATIONS

1. Without a budget and an established administrative vehicle, evaluation efforts cannot succeed to be continuous and closely linked to training programs. Evaluation should be considered as natural as administration.

2. The results of evaluation should be disseminated to all of the groups affected by a training program. Everyone should receive feedback on the training and its effects. This includes community groups, the trainees themselves, program directors and funding sources.

3. The rights of the powerless, such as clients or students, must be protected during the course of the evaluation. At no time should these rights be sacrificed for the goals of the evaluation.

VALUES

1. Values should be quantified and made explicit. The values of multiple groups, each with a different perspective, should be elicited. This includes students,

consumers and community groups. Differences between value orientations at different levels within the same organization should also be elicited. The values of schools involved in training programs are also part of the value-elicitation process.

2. Evaluation should be considered part of the administrative program at all levels and not a separate research arm.

3. The findings of evaluation should be used in continuous feedback for the subsequent decisions and actions of the administration. Evaluation research should thus be designed to influence the management and content of training programs.

4. Both inside and outside evaluators are needed in order to balance the limitations of each view.

5. Any evaluation system used should recognize the less formal and implicit values which may determine the actual choices made in the course of training.

6. There is a danger in looking only at short-term evaluation objectives. It is essential to keep a longer perspective in view, even if a long-term objective cannot be immediately measured. And the interaction of objectives must also be considered; achieving one may scuttle the rest.

7. In all evaluations, there should be room for innovation and change. No evaluation system should become closed too soon. Evaluations should change just as training programs change. They should be kept open to the input from a variety of disciplines. This is to ensure that we don't win battles but lose wars.

GOALS

Evaluation research's primary business is the elicitation of others' values and goals. Evaluation researchers should help in the classification of goals, rather than investigating their own goals.

PROCEDURES

1. Unobtrusive measurement should be used whenever possible.

2. No single scale or measure can be used in the evaluation of a training program. Multiple measurement should always be used.

3. No one set of standardized measures should be the only ones used across the board, although such variables as money or enrollment might be included in every evaluation. There should always be some measures which are tailored to the unique context, setting and people in the training program evaluated.

4. Although generally the methodological procedures used in evaluation should be consistent with the goals of evaluation, it is useful to keep the methodology loose enough so that procedures may be incorporated which may not be consistent with the stated goals. This is so unstated and implicit goals may be picked up by unorthodox means.

5. No evaluation system is forever. All evaluation systems must change. There is no single system which will be appropriate regardless of context.

EFFECTS

1. Effects are the ultimate criteria of training:

effects on trainees and particularly on clients and communities.

2. Accountability is critical in evaluation. In establishing accountability, auditing is only one step. Attaching consequences to outcomes is another. Where possible, the evaluation should be tied to rewards for valued outcomes. These may be thought of as goal or objective auditors.

3. Training in evaluation research should be provided. Such training should be multidisciplinary. Input is needed from social sciences and management sciences, as well as the traditional mental health professions. Such evaluation research training should particularly stress methods for eliciting and quantifying values and objectives. Evaluation should be considered a multidisciplinary field. Training in basic research methods is not sufficient.

4. Evaluation efforts should begin with mutual goal-setting between students, trainers, clients and community groups. If not begun with, the evaluation research should include formal consideration of the value systems and the related goals, objectives and means to attain them.

5. Evaluation researchers must recognize the importance of (1) considering the system as a whole and (2) measuring and maximizing the achievement of all the goals and objectives without the unintentional sacrifice of the values of some, or unintentional harm to the long-term objectives by concentrating on the short-term, or unintentional harm to adjoining systems; e.g., sacrificing knowledge acquisition in order to meet practical community goals. Evaluation researchers should never sacrifice complexity for simplicity or ease of measurement.

References

Arnhoff, F. N. et al. The mental health field: An overview of manpower growth and development. In F. N. Arnhoff, E. A. Rubenstein, & J. C. Speisman (Ed.), *Manpower for mental health*. Chicago: Aldine, 1969. Pp. 1–37.

Campbell, D. T. Factors relevant to the validity of experiments in social settings. In H. Schulberg, A. Sheldon, & F. Baker (Ed.), *Evaluation in health fields*. New York: Behavioral, 1969. Pp. 165–185.

Campbell, D. T. Reforms as experiments. In F. G. Caro (Ed.), *Readings in evaluation research*. New York: Russell Sage, 1971. Pp. 223–261.

Caro, F. G. (Ed.) *Readings in evaluative research*. New York: Russell Sage, 1971.

Cassels, L. Eight steps to better training: You can benefit from new ways in which adults learn. *Nation's Business*. 1961, **49**, 40ff.

Cherns, A. Social research and its diffusion. In F. G. Caro (Ed.), *Readings in evaluation research*. New York: Russell Sage, 1971. Pp. 63–71.

Cronbach, L. J. Course improvement through evaluation. *Teachers College Record,* 1963, **64**, 672, 683.

Cronbach, L. J. Evaluation for course improvement. In R. W. Heath (Ed.), *New curricula*. New York: Harper and Row, 1964.

DeLong, E. H. A philosophy of training and education for the federal service. In *Reports from the Presidential Task Force in Career Advancement*. Washington, D.C.: U. S. Government Printing Office, 1967. Pp. 56–90.

Dressel, P. L., Mayhew, L. B. Evaluation as an end to instruction. In S. J. French (Ed.), *Accent on teaching*. New York: Harper, 1954.

Edwards, W. Social utilities. Preprint of article in proceedings of a symposium, Decision and risk analysis — powerful new tools for management. U.S. Naval Academy, Annapolis, June 19, 1971.

Enelow, A. J., Adler, L. M. Organization of post-graduate courses in psychiatry. *Archives of General Psychiatry,* 1965, **12**, 433–37.

Fagin, C. Accountability. *Nursing Outlook,* 1971, **19**, 249–251.

Fergerson, F. G. Mobilization of institutional resources for change. In G. W. Manger & T. W. Briggs (Ed.), *Staff development in mental health services*. New York: National Assoc. of Social Workers, 1966. Pp. 83–98.

Freeman, H. E., & Sherwood, C. C. Large scale intervention programs. In F. G. Caro (Ed.) *Readings in evaluation research*. New York: Russell Sage, 1971. Pp. 262–276.

Gagne, R. M. *The conditions of learning*. New York: Holt, Rinehart and Winston, 1965.

Hagen, E. P., & Thorndike, R. L. Evaluation. In C. W. Harris (Ed.), *Encyclopedia of educational research*. (3rd ed.) New York: Macmillan, 1960.

Halpert, H. P. Models for the application of systems analysis to the delivery of mental health services. In D. Adelson & B. Kalis (Ed.), *Community psychology and mental health*. Scranton, Pa.: Chandler, 1970. Pp. 238–252.

Herzog, E. How much are they helped? Some notes on evaluative research. In A. J. Bindman & A. D. Spiegel (Ed.), *Perspectives in community mental health*. Chicago: Aldine, 1969. Pp. 683–693.

Hodges, A. The mental health professional in the community: Some generalizations for effectiveness. *Mental Hygiene*, 1964, **48**, 363–365.

Hume, P. B. Community psychiatry, social psychiatry and community health work: Some inter-professional relationships in psychiatry and social work. *American Journal of Psychiatry*, 1964, 340–343.

Kelly, J. G. Ecological constraints on mental health services. *American Psychologist*, 1966, **21**, 535–539.

Kelly, J. G. Toward an ecological conception of preventive intervention. In D. Adelson and B. Kalis (Ed.), *Community psychology and mental health*. Scranton, Pa.: Chandler, 1970. Pp. 126–145.

Mann, J. Technical and social difficulties in the conduct of evaluative research. In F. G. Caro (Ed.), *Readings in evaluative research*. New York: Russell Sage, 1971. Pp. 175–184.

McClelland, D. C. & Winter, D. G. *Motivating economic achievement*. New York: Free Press, 1969.

Miller, H. *Teaching and learning in adult education*. New York: Macmillan, 1964.

Pollard, W. E., & Mitchell, T. R. Decision theory analysis of social power. *Psychological Bulletin*. 78:**6,** 1972, 433–46.

Rines, A. R. Principles and purposes of evaluation. In A. R. Rines (Ed.), *Evaluating student progress in learning the practice of nursing*. New York: Columbia University Teachers College, 1963.

Schulberg, H. C., Sheldon, A., & Baker, F. (Ed.), *Evaluation in health fields*. New York: Behavioral, 1969.

Skinner, B. F., *Science and human behavior*. New York: Macmillan, 1953.

Stake, R. The countenance of educational evaluation. *Teachers College Record*, 1967, **68,** 523–540.

Suchman, E. A. *Evaluative research*. New York: Russell Sage, 1967.

Bibliography

Adelson, Daniel & Kalis, Betty, L. *Community psychology and mental health: Prospectives and challenges.* Scranton, Penn., Chandler Pub., 1970.

Adler, Peter T. Internship training for a contemporary profession of psychology, *Professional Psychologist*, 1970, *1*, (4), 371–6.

Albee, G. W. The manpower crisis in mental health. *American Journal of Public Health*, 1960, *50*, (12), 1895–1900.

Aldrich, K. C., & Bernhardt, H. Evolution of a change in teaching psychiatry to medical students. *Amer. J. of Ortho.*, 1963, (33), 105–114.

Alpine, G. C., Chester, R., Cunningham, N. K., Kaufman, N. H. Interviewing techniques for social work student training. An evaluation study of coronary care nursing training, *Mental Hygiene*, HEW.

119

Annotated Bibliography on Inservice Training for Key Professionals in Community Mental Health, #1900, U. S. Dept. of H.E.W., 1969.

Annotated Bibliography on Inservice Training for Allied Professionals and Nonprofessionals in Community Mental Health, #1901, U. S. Dept. of H.E.W., 1969.

Annotated Bibliography on Inservice Training in Mental Health for Staff in Residential Institutions, #1902, U. S. Dept. of H.E.W., 1969.

Austin, Michael J. A developmental view of the comprehensive community mental health concept. *Comm. Mental Health Journal. 5*, (2), 156–163.

Bahn, Anita K. An outline for community mental health research. *Comm. Mental Health Journal*, Spr. 1965, *1*, (1), 23–28.

Baker, Frank. An open systems approach to the study of mental hospitals in transition. *Comm. Mental Health Journal. 5* (5) 69, 403–412.

Baker, Frank & Schulberg, Herbert. The development of CHJ ideology scale. *Comm. Mental Health Journal*, 3, (3) 1967, 216–225.

Baler, A. Training for research in community mental health. *Comm. Mental Health Journal*, 1967, *3*, (3), 250–254.

Baler, A. CMH Training Programs in a school of public health. *Comm. Mental Health Journal*, 1965, *1*, (3), 238–244.

Barret, James. The case for evaluation of training expenses. *Business Horizons*, Ap. 1969, *12*, (2), 67–72.

Barton, Walter & Malamud, Wm. Training the psychiatrist to meet changing needs. American Psychiatric Assn. Washington, D. C. 1963.

Bauman, G. & Dorsey, J. Training public health nurses in mental health. *Archives of General Psychiatry*, 1964, *11*, (2),214–222.

Beitler, G. Psychiatric aide in service training: An experimental approach. *Nursing Research*, 1960, *9*, 12–16.

Belkin, M. Mental health training for the child health conference. *American J. of Health*, 1965, *55*, 1046–1056.

Bellak, L. *Handbook of community psychiatry.* New York: Grune & Stratton, 1964, (280–6) 82–122.

Bennett, C. C., Anderson, L. S., Cooper, S., Hassol, L., Klein, D. & Rosenblum, G. (Eds.) Community psychology: A report of the Boston conference on the education of psychologists for community mental health. Boston: Boston University Press, 1966.

Bennett, E. & Kaplan F. A way of thinking: Mental health professions in community programs. *Comm. Mental Health Journal*, 1967, *3*, (4), 318–324.

Bergil, L., & Cohen. *Social workers in community mental health.* Univer. of Chicago, July 1972, School of Social Service Administration.

Berker, Gilbert & Eisdorfer, Carl. Closed ranks in microcosms: Pitfalls of a training experience in consultation. *Comm. Mental Health Journal*, 1970, 6, (2), 101–109.

Bettis, M. & Roberts, R. F. The mental health manpower dilemma. *Mental Hygiene*, 1969, *53*, (1), 163–5.

Blackman, S. An evaluation of the effectiveness of a mental hygiene video presentation on adjustment. *Mental Hygiene*, 1964, (48), 633–8.

Brandon, S. & Gurenberg, E. Evaluation of community treatment programs. *The Milbank Memorial Fund Quarterly*, 1966, *44*, 11–395.

Breiter, D. E., Golann, S. M. & Magoon, T. M. A filmed interview applied to the evaluation of mental health counselors. *Psychotherapy: Theory, Research and Practice.* 1966, 3, 21–24.

Brigante, Thomas R. Opportunities for community mental health training within the residential college camp. *Comm. Mental Health Journal*, Spring 1965, *1*, (1), 55–60.

Brigante, Thomas. The assessment process in campus community mental health programs. *Comm. Mental Health Journal*, 1969, *5*, (2), 140–148.

Byrns, L. & Crane, D. Training by objectives. *Training and Development Journal*, June 1969, *23*, (3), 38–48.

Carter, J. W. Jr. *Research contributions from psychology to community mental health*. Behavioral Publications, 1968.

Chaplan, Abraham, Price, John Jr. & Zuckerman, Isadore. The role of volunteers in community mental health programs. *Comm. Mental Health Journal*, 1966, *2*, (3), 255–258.

Clements, Wm., Kaplan, M. & Kurtox, R. Psychiatric residents and lower class patients: Conflict in training. *Comm. Mental Health Journal*, 1968, *4*, (1), 91–94.

Cochron, M. A., Steiner, K. E. Evaluation of an in-service training program using the SREB information test. *Amer. Journal of Mental Deficiency*, May 1966, *70*, 913–917.

Cohen, R. & Schulberg, H. A review and preview of a training program in community mental health. 1970, *Comm. Mental Health Journal*, *6*, (5), 383–386.

Cole, Charles & Hinkle, J., Oetting, E. R. Research in a community health clinic: A framework for action. *Comm. Mental Health Journal*, 1968, *4*, (2), 129–133.

Community Mental Health Nursing. *A Journal of Nursing*, 1970, *10*, (5),1019–1021.

Cooper, Morton & Southard, Curtis. The mental health exchange: An important function of a community mental health center. *Comm. Mental Health Journal*, Winter, 1966, *2*, (4), 343–345.

Cowen, E. L. Combined graduate-undergraduate training in community mental health. *Professional Psychology*, 1969, *1*, 72–77.

Cowen, E. L. Combined graduate-undergraduate training in community mental health. *Professional Psychology*, Nov. 1969, 1 (1),72–73.

Cowen, E., Chinsky, L., & Rappaport J. An undergraduate practicum in community mental health. *Comm. Mental Health Journal*, 1970, *6*, (2), 91–100.

Cowen, E. L. Training clinical psychologists for community mental functions: description of a practicum experience. In I. Iscoe & C. D. Spielberger (Eds.) *Training and Research in Community Mental Health*. New York: Appleton-Century-Crofts, 1970, pp. 99–124.

DeGroot, J. C. & Gottschalk, L. A. & Whitman, R. N. An evaluation of a program of continuing education in community mental health. *Comprehensive Psychiatry*, 1969, *10*, (6), 423–442.

Distefano, M. K. Jr., & Pryer, M. W. Evaluating the training of psychiatric attendants. *Mental Hygiene*, July 1965, *49*, (1), 347–350.

Distefano, M. K., & Poe, M. B. & Pryer, M. W. Effects of training programs on psychiatric attendance. *Mental Hygiene*, 1966, *51*, 66–70.

Distefano, M. K., & Marr, L. W. & Pryer, M. W. Attitude change in psychiatric attendants following experience and training, *Mental Hygiene*, April 1969, *53*, (2), 253–257.

Distefano, M. J. Jr. & Pryer, M. W. Stability of attitudes in psychiatric attendants following training. *Mental Hygiene*, July 1970, *54*,(3), 433–435.

Dobbsin, J. & Dorgan, R. E. A descriptive analysis of the mental health program worker training project. *International Journal of Social Psychiatry*, 1970, *16*,(4), 288–293.

Downing, J. J., & Heymann, G. W. Some initial approaches to continuous evaluation of a county mental health program: An interim report. *Journal of Public Health*, AGI (51) 980–989.

Edelson, Marshall & Lidz, Theodore, *Training tomorrow's psychiatrist: The crisis in curriculum*. New Haven: Yale University Press, 1970.

Edwards, A. L. & Cronbach, L. J. Experimental design for research in psychotherapy. *Journal of Clinical Psychology*, 1952, *8*, 51–59.

Eisdorfer, Carl & Golann, Stuart. Principles for the training of "new professions" in mental health. *Comm. Mental Health Journal* 1969, *5* (5), 349–357.

Ellison, David & Hessler, Richard & Hitchcock, John. Problem in developing a community based research component for a mental health center. *Mental Hygiene*, July 1971, *55*, (3), 312–317.

Esty, Jonathan, Jarvis, Paul & Stutzman, Leon. Evaluation and treatment of families at the Fort Logan Mental Health Center. *Comm. Mental Health Journal.* 1969, *5*, (1), 14–19.

Evans, Phyllis P., & Bracht, Neil F. Meeting social works challenge in community mental health. *Mental Hygiene*, 1971, *55*, (3), 295–297.

Fox, P.D. & Kuldan, J.M. Expanding the framework for mental health program evaluations. *Archives of General Psychiatry*, 1968, *19*,(5), 538–544.

Freed, Harvey, M. & Miller, Louis. Planning a community mental health program: A case history. *Comm. Mental Health Journal*, 1971, 7, (2), 107–117.

Geis, G. & Tenney, C. W. Jr. Evaluating a training institute for juvenile court judges. *Comm. Mental Health Journal*, 1968, *4*, (6),461–468.

Gross, Zoltan. The social content of training psychotherapists: Trends in the social role of the therapist and in the demand for his services. In Holt, R. *New Horizons for Psychotherapy*, 1971, New York International Universities Press, 81–104.

Geisman, L. B., Krisberg, J. & Ludwig, L. Trained vs. untrained workers in services to individual and families. In Geisman, L. (Ed.) *The Forgotten Neighborhood*. Metuchen, N.J.: Scarecrow Press, 1967.

Gilbert, D. & Levinson, D. Ideology, personality and institutional policy in the mental hospital. *J. of Abnormal and Social Psychiatry*, 1956, (53).

Goldfarb, Allan. Current mental health program evaluation in San Mateo County. *Comm. Mental Health Journal*, Fall 1967, 3, (3), 285–289.

Goldston, S. E. Training in community psychiatry. A survey report of the medical school department of psychiatry. *Am. J. of Psychiatry*, 1964, (20), 789–792.

Gottesfeld, H., Rhee, C. & Parker, G. A study of the role of paraprofessionals in community mental health. *Comm. Mental Health Journal*, 6, (4), 1970, 285–291.

Greenberg, E. M. Evaluating the effectiveness of community health services, New York Mental Health Material Center, 1966.

Greenfield, H. N., Miller, M. H., Roberts, L. M. *Comprehensive mental health: The challenge of evaluation.* Madison: University of Wisconsin Press, 1968, 339.

Guidelines for evaluation of continuing education programs in mental health. National Clearinghouse for Mental Health Information. NIMH. April 22–23, 1969.

Hadley, John & Kepas, S. An experiment in the education of the professional health worker. The Purdue program. *Comm. Mental Health Journal*, 1970, 6 (1), 40–50.

Haid, D. M. Teaching of psychiatric aides. In Redmond, M. J. & Drake, M. E. (Eds.) *Teaching and Implementation of Psychiatric Mental Health Nursing.* Washington, D.C.: The Catholic Univ. Press, 1958, 160–176.

Hansell, M. & Wodarczyk, M. & Visotsky, H. The mental health expediter: A review after 2 years of the project and one year of the expediter in action. *Archives of General Psychiatry*, 1968, 18, 392–399.

Harris, M., Kinegman, G. & Rosinski, E. A continuous educational program for paramedical personnel. *Comm. Mental Health Journal*, 1968, 4, (5), 377–387.

Herzog, Allen, Levy, Leo, & Slotkin, Elizabeth. The evaluation of state wide mental health programs: A systems approach. *Comm. Mental Health Journal*, 1968, *4*, (4) 340–349.

Herzog, Allen N, & Levy, Leo. The birth and demise of a planning unit in a state mental health department. *Comm. Mental Health Journal*, 1971,7, (8), 198–203.

Hill, Richard J. Graduate Research Training in Sociology. A Preliminary Report. Purdue University, May 1970.

Hunter, Wm. & Ratcliffe, Allen. The range mental health center evaluation of a community oriented mental health consultation program in northern Minnesota. *Comm. Mental Health Journal*, 1968, *4*, (3), 260–268.

Hutcheson, Bellenden R., & Krause, Elliott A. Systems analysis and mental health services. *Comm. Mental Health Journal*, 1967, *5*, (1), 29–45.

Iscoe, Ira & Spielberger, Charles D. The current status of training in community psychology. In Iscoe, Ira & Spielberger, Charles D.(Eds.) *Community Psychology: Perspectives in Training and Research*. New York: Appleton-Century-Crofts, 1970.

Iscoe, Ira and Spielberger, Charles D. Graduate education in community psychology, *Handbook of Community Mental Health*, Stuart, E., Golann, S. E., & Eisdorser, C. (eds.), 1972 New York: Appleton-Century-Crofts, 909–920.

James, G. Evaluation in public health practice. *Amer. J. of Public Health*, 1962, *52*, 1145–1154.

James, G. Evaluation in public health service. *Amer. J. of Public Health*, 1962, *5*, (7), 145–154.

Keith-Spiegel, Patricia & Spiegel, Donald E. Effects of mental hospital experiences on attitudes of teen age students toward mental illness. *J. of Clinical Psychology*, 1970, *26*, (3), 387–388.

Kelly, James G. Antidotes for arrogance: Training for community psychology. *American Psychologist*, 1970,

25,(6).

Kelly, James G. Qualities for the community psychologist. *American Psychologist*, Oct. 1971, *26*, (10).

Lamb, Richard H., Heath, Don & Downing, Joseph I. *Handbook of community mental health practice*. San Francisco: Jossey Bass, Inc., 1969.

Langston, Robert. Community mental health centers and community mental health ideology. *Comm. Mental Health Journal*, 1970, *6*, (5), 387–392.

Lehmann, Stanley. Community and Psychology and community psychology. *American Psychologist*, June 1971, *26*, (6), 554–560.

Lipsitt, Paul & Stienbruner, Maureen. An experiment on police-community relations: A small group approach. *Comm. Mental Health Journal*, 1969, *5*, (2), 172–179.

Lynch, Mary & Gardner, Elmer A. Some issues raised in the training of a paraprofessional personnel as clinic therapists. *Amer. J. of Psychiatry*, 1970, *126*, (10), 1473–1479.

MacLennan, B.W., Klein, W., Pearl, A., & Fishman, J. Training for new careers. *Comm. Mental Health Journal*, Summer 1966, *2*, (2), 135–141.

MacMahon, Brian, Pugt, Thomas & Hutchson, George. Principles in the evaluation of community mental health programs. *Journal of Public Health*, July 1961, *51*, (7), 963–968.

Madore, C. E. & McLeigh, L. R. & Newman, F. L. & Sears, W. *Training nonprofessional community project leaders*. New York: Behavioral Publications, 1970.

Magner, George W. Evaluation of the leadership training program. In Magner, G. (Ed.) *Leadership training in Mental Health*.

Mann, L., Wright, T., Hichsendager, D. & Harold J. A pilot training program to develop physical recreation leaders for work with emotionally disturbed children.

Comm. Mental Health Journal, Summer 1967, *3*, (2), 159–162.

Mathews, Wm. A research evaluation of an action approach to school mental health workshop, *Amer. J. of Ortho.*, 1961, 31, 320–346.

McAllistor, L. W. Olson, Polley, G. W. & Wilson, K. P. Mental health training for county welfare social work personnel: an exercise in education and community organization. *Comm. Mental Health Journal,* 1971, *7*, (1), 29–38.

McGee, Thomas F. & Wolfe, J. B. Patterns of community mental health development in major American cities. *Comm. Mental Health Journal,* 1972, *8*, (1) 17–27.

Moss, Rudolph & Otto, Jean. Community oriented programs. Environment scale: A methodology for facilitation. Evaluation of social change. *Comm. Mental Health Journal,* 1972, *8*, (1), 28, 37.

Moss, Rudolph. Assessment of the psychosocial environment of community-oriented psychiatric treatment programs. *J. of Abnormal Psych.* 1972, *19*, (1), 9–18.

Murrell, Stanley. Community involvement in mental health programs. *Comm. Mental Health Journal,* 1969, *5*, (1), 82–87.

Osterkil, Jerry. Evaluation: A keystone of comprehensive health planning, *Comm. Mental Health Journal,* 1969, *5*, (2), 121–126.

Pasemonk, Richard & Rardin, Max. Theoretical models in community mental health. *Mental Hygiene*, July 1971, *55*, (3), 358–364.

Pattison, Mansell. Residency training issues in community psychiatry. Unpublished paper.

Pattison, Mansell. Community mental health, education and training program model. Assoc. Professor, University of California. Unpublished paper.

Pattison, Mansell, Elpers, John. A development view of

mental health manpower trends. 5th World congress of psychiatry and 125th annual meeting. American Psychiatric Association.

Pattison Mansell. Group psychotherapy and group methods in community mental health programs. *Int. J. of Group Psychotherapy*, 1970, 20, (4), 516–539.

Phillips, Leslie. The competence criterion for mental health programs. *Comm. Mental Health Journal*, Spring 1967, *3*, (1), 73–76.

Polley, George W. & McAllistor, Loring W., & Olson, Ted. W., & Wilson, Karen P. Mental health training for county welfare social work personnel: An exercise in education and community organization. *Comm. Mental Health Journal*, March 1971, 7, (1), 29–38.

Powell, Thomas & Riley, John. The basic elements of community mental health education. *Comm. Mental Health Journal*, 1970, *6*, (3), 196–202.

Riessman, Frank. Strategies and suggestions for training nonprofessionals. *Comm. Mental Health Journal,*, 1967, *3*, (2), 103–110.

Rioch, Margaret, J. N.I.M.H. study in training mental health counselors. *American Journal of Orthopsychiatry*, 1963, *33*, 678–689.

Rioch, Margaret J. Changing concepts in the training of therapists. *Journal of Consulting Psychology*, 1966, *30* (4), 290–292.

Rogawski, Alexander S. Community psychiatry and the education of psychiatrists. *Comm. Mental Health Journal*, 1969, *5*, (2), 129–139.

Ross, Eleanor R., & Reiff R., & Zusman, Jack. Evaluation of the quality of mental health services. *Archives of General Psychiatry*, March 1969, *20*, (3), 352–357.

Scott, P. A. & Signell, M. A. Training in consultation: A crisis in role transition. *Comm. Mental Health Journal*, 1972, *8*, (2), 149–160.

Shore, Milton & Mannino, Fortune V. *Mental health and the community: Problems, programs, strategies.* New York: Behavioral Publications, 1969.

Singer, G. L. The social workers role in a community mental health program. *Hospital and Community Psychiatry*, 1971, 22, (8), 246–247.

Smith, Wm., & Harnell, Norris. Territorial evaluation of mental health services. *Comm. Mental Health Journal*, 1969, *3* (2), 19–124.

Smith, Wm., & Hobbs, Nicholas. The community and the community mental health center. APA Inc., June, 1966 (24).

Spiegal, Hans B. C. Changing assumptions about community change. *Journal of Community Development*, 1971, *2*, (2), 5–15.

Terral, David L., McWilliams, Spencer A., & Cowen, Emory L. Description and evaluation of group work training for nonprofessional aides in a school. *Psychology in the School*, Jan., 1972, *9*, (1), 70–75.

Toban, Eileen. Perceived skill of professional and nonprofessional community health workers. *J. of Consulting and Clinical Psychology*, 1970, *34*, (3), 308–313.

Tracey, Wm. R. *Evaluating training and development systems.* New York: American Management Assn. Inc., 1968, 304.

Turner, F., & Watterloo, L. Social work in the seventies in mental health. *Canada Mental Health*, 1971, *19*, (1), 12–16.

Visotsky, Harold. Modern approaches to community mental health. *J. of Current Psychiatric Therapies*, 1970, *10*, 203–224.

Watters, T. A. *Continuing education programs in psychiatry and their evaluation.* Boulder, Col.: Western Interstate Commission for Higher Education, December 1964.

Yolles, I. The role of the psychologist in comprehensive mental health center. The National Institute of Mental Health. *American Psychologist*, 1966, *21*, 37–41.

Zacker, J., Rutter, E., & Bard, M. Evaluation of attitudinal changes in a program of community consultation. *C.M.H.J.*, 1971, *7*, (3), 236–241.